DATE		

ANIMALSCAM

ANIMALSCAM

The Beastly Abuse of Human Rights

KATHLEEN MARQUARDT

With Herbert M. Levine and Mark LaRochelle

Regnery Gateway
Washington, D.C.

Library of Congress Cataloging-in-Publication Data

Marquardt, Kathleen, 1944–
AnimalScam : the beastly abuse of human rights / Kathleen
Marquardt with Herbert M. Levine and Mark LaRochelle.
p.   cm.
Includes bibliographical references and index.
ISBN 0-89526-498-6 (acid-free paper)
1. Animal rights activists—United States.   2. Animal rights
movement—United States.   3. Radicals—United States.   I. Levine,
Herbert M.   II. LaRochelle, Mark, 1959–   .   III. Title.   IV. Title:
Animal scam.
HV4764.M225   1993
179'.3—dc20   93-24500
                                                        CIP

Published in the United States by
Regnery Gateway, Inc.
1130 17th Street, NW
Washington, DC 20036

Distributed to the trade by
National Book Network
4720-A Boston Way
Lanham, MD 20706

Printed on acid-free paper.

Manufactured in the United States of America.

10 9 8 7 6 5 4 3 2 1

DEDICATION

This book is dedicated to all the victims of animal extremism:

• wild animals suffering and dying from overpopulation, disease, and habitat degradation because of irrational attacks on hunting, trapping, and wildlife management

• endangered species becoming extinct because of irrational attacks on captive breeding, veterinary research and rehabilitation, and private propagation

• pets abandoned or killed because of excessive licensing fees and unjust restrictions on pet ownership and shelter adoption

• hunters, trappers and their families, who are subject to harassment and violence, and deprived of their livelihoods, recreation, and source of meat

• farmers and ranchers, who face increasingly crippling over-regulation and attacks, and livestock and crop depredation from overpopulated predators and pests

• biomedical researchers who brave unbelievable terror to find treatments and cures to save both people and animals

• the hungry, who bear artificially high food costs because of restrictions on agriculture and prohibitions on the donation of game to charity

• patients who have died, and those now suffering, because of research delays caused by absurd regulatory burdens and terrorist assaults on biomedical laboratories

• and finally, this book is dedicated to all the world's children and animals, who will live longer, healthier lives through the mutually beneficial symbiosis of man and animals, once the extremist threat is eliminated.

ACKNOWLEDGEMENTS

Thanks to Al Regnery for the courage to publish this book, deemed not "politically correct" by other publishers. The authors have the honor to have written the first book ever to have generated hate mail to Regnery even before publication. Our gratitude also goes out to our agent, Audrey Wolf, and to Ed Artinian, who suggested Regnery. Thanks also to Megan Butler, Jennifer Reist, and our editor Trish Bozell, and to the many specialists around the country who reviewed the manuscript for factual accuracy. And to Bill Wewer, for countless hours editing, proofing, vetting, and improving the manuscript, no amount of thanks can be enough.

We appreciate the extraordinary effort of the overworked and undermanned staff of Putting People First, particularly David W. Almasi, Judith Zahnd, M. J. McGraw, and Richard C. Nearing. And special thanks to the countless individual members and supporters of Putting People First who sent us the information compiled in this book, and invited us to visit their farms, laboratories, refuges, and more, despite incredible threats and intimidation. Without our grassroots network, this book would not have been possible. Thanks to their tireless legwork, there will come a day when we can publicly thank them all by name without fear of terrorist retaliation.

Whatever is of value in this book is due to the generous assistance of these fine people. All errors are solely the fault of the authors.

CONTENTS

PART 3

DANGER AND OPPORTUNITY: THE THREAT TO HUMAN RIGHTS AND HOW TO FIGHT BACK

INTRODUCTION: WHY I WROTE THIS BOOK
Mommy, We're Murderers!

"Mommy, she said you're a murderer," cried my daughter Montana. The "she," I learned, was a representative from People for the Ethical Treatment of Animals (PeTA).[1] For three days, she had lectured my daughter and her seventh-grade classmates about "animal rights." One of the lessons was that all hunters are murderers.

What in the world was animal rights? I wondered.

As someone who grew up on a small farm out west, I am appalled that anybody would accuse me and other hunters of being murderers merely because we prefer to provide our own food whenever possible. Eighteen million Americans—about the same number of people who live in the entire state of New York—hunt, and they are not murderers; neither am I.

I told Montana that I sent her and her sister to school to learn, not to be brainwashed. How many other lies had this PeTA outsider told our schoolchildren over the past three days?

To protect my children, I wanted to learn everything there was to know about animal rights. I began to talk about it with my husband, Bill Wewer, a lawyer. At one time, the Doris Day Animal League had been a client of his, but he had only done tax and corporate work for them, not issues, so he didn't know much more than I about what animal rights advocates believed.

At just that time, I developed a serious health problem. While scuba diving in the Caribbean over Christmas 1989, I came down with a mysterious infection. For eight months I suffered painful symptoms as well as headaches so bad I had to take codeine. After endless tests, my doctors finally identified my illness as Giardia, complicated by amoebic dysentery. I was cured by a megadose of

Atabrine (a medicine used for malaria) and a twelve-week series of antibiotics.

While I was laid up, I read everything I could find on animal rights. I learned of activists who picket zoos, circuses, rodeos, pet shops, medical research centers, and fur salons. I saw them engage in "hunter harassment." I saw them infiltrate legitimate animal welfare organizations and take them over for animal rights purposes. And I saw them lobby for restrictions to make it difficult, if not impossible, for people to own or use animals.

I discovered that this movement is not about animal shelters or veterinary care; it is an attempt to outlaw an unfathomably large chunk of our economy—everything from animal research to pets.

And I saw something else—zealots who intimidate their opponents, often crossing the line between legitimate protest and crime. These borderline radicals make menacing telephone calls, send unordered merchandise to people's homes (which hurts the merchant, not the recipient), harass women wearing furs by splattering red paint or glue on their coats, and intimidate researchers with death threats or bomb scares. I since have been on the receiving end of much of this myself. Even my children's lives have been threatened. I learned that such threats often give way to actual terrorism.

Still recuperating from my illness, I read of one case that exposed animal rights in a way that really hit home. On April 2, 1989, a group called the Animal Liberation Front (ALF) destroyed the laboratory of a researcher at the University of Arizona in Tucson. Equipment was vandalized, two buildings were destroyed by gasoline fires, and $300,000 in damage was inflicted.

Over one thousand animals were stolen, including many being used to study osteoporosis, cystic fibrosis, heart disease, and cancer. Also released were mice infected with cryptosporidium, a protozoan that causes fatal child dysentery in the Third World and is known to be fatal to AIDS patients. The animals had been raised in a temperature-controlled facility, but were "liberated" to a desert in which temperatures exceeded 100 degrees and where they faced agonizing death from dehydration.[2]

This attack was mild compared to some I will describe in the following pages. But as a result of this one, a respected parasitologist quit working on a project on lethal parasites similar to mine. And he was not the only scientist to abandon important medical research in the face of threats by animal rights activists. I wondered about the people suffering from those diseases. Were they to be sacrificed in the name of rats?

And I learned that the organization acting as mouthpiece for the ALF terrorists was PeTA, the very group that had conducted the seminar in my daughter's school![3] With a shock I realized that my children were being indoctrinated by a group that supported life-threatening terrorism.

If these people want to live on tofu and sprouts, wear plastic clothes, and refuse medical treatment, that is their business. They have a right to preach the virtues of a paleolithic lifestyle, and to try to persuade others to join them in worshiping rats and bugs. But when they turn to violence, and subvert public education to indoctrinate children into these ideas, they have gone too far.

Recognizing a problem and doing something about it are two different things. It was easy to say, "Somebody has got to do something about this" and leave the work to somebody else. I was no different from most people. We get on with our daily lives, putting aside concerns that seem too large for us. But sometimes we must redirect our energies to deal with a public menace.

Candy Lightner is one case in point. In 1980, she was incensed to learn that the drunken driver who killed her thirteen-year-old daughter had been convicted of drunk driving and related offenses three times in four years. He had served only forty-eight hours in jail. So she formed Mothers Against Drunk Driving (MADD), an organization committed to preventing the tragedy that had devastated her family from being repeated and devastating the lives of others. Since then, MADD has been responsible for a great deal of legislation and education against drunk driving, saving the lives of countless people.

I too felt a responsibility to act. I told my husband, "There comes a point in life when you have to give something back. We live a great life. We hunt, fish, ski, scuba dive, and travel. We have two super children. This country has been good to us. It's time to give something back."

Bill agreed. We decided to find some organization challenging the animal rightists. We went to the sportsmen's clubs, farm groups, pet fanciers, and professional and trade associations, but found that even when they were active, they were mostly defensive—responding to the animal rights groups rather than initiating campaigns.

Even worse, each group was combating animal rights from its own narrow outlook rather than from an all-encompassing perspective, and consequently, continually reinventing the wheel.

Most distressing of all, each group was so specialized that it was just as ignorant as any layman when it came to other animal-use groups. While they all knew the animal rightists were lying about them, they were inclined to give the activists the benefit of the doubt when they attacked others. Most people have been programmed to believe lies from an "activist" before truth from a "vested interest."

I met biomedical and veterinary researchers who passionately defended their attempts to alleviate the pain and suffering of people and animals, but who believed hunters were barbaric. Hunters would explain in detail their role in conservation, but thought farmers had no similar concern. And farmers patiently explained how their livelihood depended on the well-being of their animals, but believed that biomedical researchers "tortured" their animals. I met researchers, wildlife biologists, and agricultural scientists, all at the same university, who never spoke to each other! We were being destroyed by a "divide and conquer" strategy. We were fighting a limited war on the defensive, against an enemy who is conducting a total war on the offensive.

When you negotiate with animal rightists, they bring nothing to the table but demands; they view any compromise as weakness. They will take everything they can get now, but they will not stop there. Animal rightists will never be satisfied with anything short of the total abolition of all animal use.

A rational person does not negotiate with a gun to his head. When someone says, "We will bury you," the proper response is not, "How can I help?" The proper response is to start forging alliances.

When he inscribed his signature to the Declaration of Independence, it is said that Ben Franklin warned, "We must hang together, else assuredly we shall hang separately." Hunters are just 7 percent of our population, farmers a mere 2 percent, and researchers a tiny fraction of that. Even if every person in each particular segment were to get active, none could stand alone. But together, from pet fanciers to patients, we are 96 percent of mankind.

So far as I could see, no group represented ordinary citizens, or was willing to take on and expose the animal rights crowd as the frauds they are.

I became more committed than ever to expose the ugly truth about animal rights. In March of 1990, with Bill's help, I incorporated Putting People First,[4] a national nonprofit organization that promotes human rights, animal welfare, and conservation.

The goal of Putting People First is to recognize the unique role of man as the only earthly creature able to care about animal welfare, understand ecology, or foresee the consequences of our actions. We accept our responsibility as stewards of animals and the earth, without running away from it. We firmly believe that only man can husband animals and other resources to the benefit of people, animals, and our common environment.

Putting People First does not mean wiping out everything else on the planet for the benefit of humans. We do not represent any industry or special interest. We are dedicated to preserving the rights of people to own and use animals and other resources humanely and responsibly, and to the sustainable development of earth's resources to enhance the quality of life for generations to come. We believe that resource management policy should be based not on emotion, ideology, or fund-raising expediency but on science, experience, and common sense.

Putting People First works to expose the dangers of extremist groups that promote the interests of animals over people and that want to outlaw all use and ownership of animals. Unlike them, we are an animal welfare group. We want animals to be treated humanely: we abhor cruelty to animals. But in stark contrast to the animal rights organizations, we believe that people should benefit from nature's surplus. We hold that humans are part of nature and the food chain, not hostile aliens who must be eradicated.

When Putting People First started, I hoped to devote half my days to the organization and half to my art and home life. But my hope of part-time involvement with the animal rights issue was short-lived. Within two or three weeks of beginning Putting People First, I was working fifty hours a week on animal rights, struggling with fashion designs in my studio on weekends and evenings, and squeezing family time in between. I was overwhelmed by my new work.

Putting People First was totally different from any group Bill and I had ever worked with. We didn't use direct mail campaigns to look for members—news about us spread by word of mouth. Within weeks, we were flooded with calls from volunteers—farmers, hunters, wildlife biologists, zoologists, breeders, circus people, veterinarians, pet fanciers, medical researchers, doctors, nurses, patients, and just plain people asking, "Where have you been? What can I do?"

Three years later, we have about forty thousand members and supporters, as well as many professional and trade associations backing us. Most of our members are in the United States and Canada but others come from every continent on earth. The animal rights movement started in Europe, but it is hurting people in Asia, Africa, Australia, and throughout North and South America. Animal rights is an international threat.

It's nice to be needed, but we had to become a full-fledged organization almost overnight, which is not easy. We had to get involved in so many different things at the same time. We lobbied for legislation, wrote *amicus* briefs for court cases, and started an opinion column within three months of the birth of our organization. At last count, the weekly column was going to over 2,000 newspapers, magazines, radio and TV stations, businesses, other groups, and government officials throughout North America and Europe.

And we gave speeches. I give approximately one hundred speeches a year, and my staff fill in when I'm booked up. While death threats arrive with the daily mail, the speeches are what once threatened to be my undoing. Before I started Putting People First I was a recluse, afraid to stand up in front of an audience. Now I speechify at the drop of a hat, though my knees remain somewhat wobbly!

This book is my attempt to spread the message of animal welfare to an even broader audience. A comprehensive story of the dangers of the animal rights movement must be told; people must learn how radically animal rights contradicts animal welfare, conservation, and human rights.

Most of all, I want to restore trust and civility between neighbors. When you know someone is lying about you, take with a grain of salt what they say about others. Don't take anyone's accusation at face value—investigate the facts for yourself. If we remember to grant the accused the presumption of innocence, and put the burden of proof on the accuser, we will not only defeat the animal rights inquisition, but go a long way toward restoring domestic tranquility.

PART ONE

ANIMAL RIGHTS: UNCOVERING THE SCAM

1

WHAT IS ANIMAL RIGHTS?
Animal Rights 101

The modern animal rights movement traces its philosophical origins to the 1975 book *Animal Liberation* by Peter Singer, a philosopher of "bioethics" in Australia, who later authored the article on "Ethics" for *The Encyclopaedia Britannica*. In *Animal Liberation* he writes, "Surely there will be some nonhuman animals whose lives, by any standards, are more valuable than the lives of some humans."[1] But which humans, and who should decide?

In 1983, Singer edited a British collection of animal rights essays called *In Defence of Animals*. In one essay, "The Case for Animal Rights," Tom Regan asks, "What could be the basis of our having more inherent value than animals? Their lack of reason, or autonomy, or intellect? Only if we are willing to make the same judgment in the case of humans who are similarly deficient."[2]

His meaning was explained in the question-and-answer session following a 1989 speech. An audience member asked Regan, if he were aboard a lifeboat with a baby and a dog, and the boat capsized, which would he rescue, the baby or the dog? Regan replied, "If it were a retarded baby and a bright dog, I'd save the dog."[3]

Such assertions may seem like a philosopher's game to most people, but this ideology has given rise to a political movement of increasing fanaticism. The motto of People for the Ethical Treatment of Animals (PeTA), the acknowledged leader of the animal movement, is "Animals are not ours to eat, wear, experiment on, or use in entertainment."

Animal rights is against *all* animal use—even to save lives.[4] It

3

seeks to ban all animal ownership or use, no matter how humane. The breadth of this ambition—what I call "animal apartheid"—is staggering.

It means no hunting, fishing, or trapping. No livestock farming or ranching. No use of animals in science or education; no animal bone marrow to treat blood disorders, or animal blood to treat Rh factor types. No beef, pork, lamb, chicken, fish, eggs, or even honey. No leather shoes, fur collars, wool sweaters, down jackets or comforters, or even silk.[5]

And this just scratches the surface. No zoos, aquariums, circuses, rodeos, horse racing, carriage rides, or animal actors in films. No butter, cheese, yogurt, or Ben & Jerry's Rainforest Crunch ice cream. No meat-byproducts in your dog and cat food—not that it makes any difference, because there would be no pets.[6]

And more: Candies, crayons, gelatin, marshmallows, drywall, home insulation, linoleum, candles, soap, glue, brake fluid, and heart valves—even the runway foam used for aircraft with disabled landing gear—all would be forbidden under an animal rights regime.

Make no mistake about it: animal rights means no milk for our children, no insulin for diabetics, and no guide dogs for the blind.[7] No rat traps could mean the return of the bubonic plague. No pest control means widespread malaria. No whole-animal models means that biomedical researchers will be hamstrung trying to control such epidemics.

Yet this movement has become a multimillion dollar industry supported by many Hollywood celebrities, from Candice Bergen to Kim Basinger—who make their fabulous incomes on film emulsion, an animal product.

Animal rights is a disaster not just for humanity, but for animals as well. It rejects the concept of animal welfare. That means no wildlife management, veterinary medicine, or captive breeding of endangered species. It means needless suffering and death for both people and animals, and even the extinction of some species. Animal rights is not out to improve animal care but to abolish it.

PeTA's former general counsel, Gary Francione, has admitted, "The theory of animal rights simply is not consistent with the theory of animal welfare. . . . Animal rights means dramatic social changes for humans and non-humans alike; if our bourgeois values prevent us from accepting those changes, then we have no right to call ourselves advocates of animals rights."[8]

Elsewhere, Francione and Tom Regan wrote, "Not only are the philosophies of animal rights and animal welfare separated by irreconcilable differences . . . the enactment of animal welfare measures actually impedes the achievement of animals rights." They concluded that "welfare reforms, by their very nature, can only serve to retard the pace at which animal rights goals are achieved."[9]

The animal rights movement is not motivated by the values shared by proponents of animal welfare. As Peter Singer writes of himself and his wife, "We were not especially 'interested in' animals. Neither of us had ever been inordinately fond of dogs, cats, or horses in the way that many people are. We didn't 'love' animals."[10]

This attitude is hard for those of us who do love animals to understand. What are these people really after?

Animal rights promotes the idea that people should have no more rights than animals. As PeTA cofounder and national director Ingrid Newkirk put it, "I don't believe human beings have the 'right to life.' That's a supremacist perversion. A rat is a pig is a dog is a boy."[11]

This ideology raises some interesting questions. For starters, why do people even think about rights? Because "rights" is a concept, and man is the only species on earth with the intellect to grasp concepts.[12]

The most important concepts people think about concern morality and ethics, questions of "right and wrong." Our unique ability to ask ethical questions and make moral choices (rather than be ruled by instinct) makes us moral agents.

Rights are the boundaries between moral agents. In order to possess rights, we must accept responsibilities to respect others' rights. We are justified in demanding our rights so long as we do not violate the rights of another moral agent.

Because animals act instinctively, they cannot even conceive of responsibilities. When a cat kills a canary, you and I may be upset, but we also understand that the nature of cats is to kill birds. We recognize that the cat has committed no moral violation. The same is true even when a lion or chimpanzee kills another member of its own species. We understand that nature has endowed animals with certain features that sometimes seem cruel. But, quite properly, we do not judge animals on a moral scale.

On the other hand, a person who torments a cat to death the way a cat might torment a mouse deserves our moral condemnation—not because cats have rights, but because people have responsibilities. Likewise, we insist it is wrong for people to burn books, deface a masterpiece, or desecrate a church—not because these things have rights, but because people have responsibilities.[13]

Rights are a serious business. They are the linchpin of a free society. Without them, people would not be able to go about their business free from arbitrary interference by government. Rights offer a people freedom to convince others of different points of view without having to resort to violence and the resulting breakdown of civilization.

The animal rights movement would allow people no more rights than rats or cockroaches. The real agenda of this movement is not to give rights to animals, but to take rights from people—to dictate our food, clothing, work, recreation, and whether we will discover new medications or die. Animal rights pose an extraordinary threat to our health, freedom, and even our lives.

Even if the use of animals in biomedical research were to produce a cure for AIDS, says Ingrid Newkirk of PeTA, "we'd be against it."[14] The reason? Mankind has "grown like a cancer. We're the biggest problem on the face of the Earth."[15] But most disturbing of all was her quote in the *Washington Post* in 1983: "Six million people died in concentration camps, but six billion broiler chickens will die this year in slaughterhouses."[16]

The inevitable consequences of Newkirk's ideology were revealed by Hermann Göring, who was head of the German Humane Society and Environmental Minister for the Third Reich. In a radio broadcast on August 18, 1933, Göring announced "an absolute and permanent ban on vivisection." For violation of his ban, he said, any "culprit shall be lodged in a concentration camp." (See chapter 10.)

By pretending to extend rights to animals, which by nature are incapable of moral cognition, the Nazis ultimately annihilated the very concept of "rights." And, as is demonstrated in this book, just as the dogma of animal rights led to the destruction of human rights under Naziism, it leads to the destruction of human rights today.

Most donors to animal rights groups would be horrified to learn of this connection. In fact, the average contributor eats meat, owns pets, wears leather, and uses medicines developed through animal research. Few realize that their donations are actually used to attack these things, to lobby for restrictions and bans on them, or merely to line the pockets of some of the movement's leaders.

Publicly, animal rights leaders disguise their agenda, distracting misguided animal lovers from the movement's true goals with a continual barrage of sensational (and generally fraudulent) allegations of animal abuse. These pages are filled with examples showing that the animal rights movement survives on deceit and misrepresentation. It cannot be stated strongly enough: every time animal rights leaders open their mouths, they lie.

Respected animal welfare groups and humane societies, moreover, are being seduced by the fund-raising potential of this radical ideology. Even the Humane Society of the United States (HSUS) has adopted the animal rights party line that "there is no rational basis for maintaining a moral distinction between the treatment of humans and other animals."[17] (Actually, HSUS is not what most of us think of as the "Humane Society." That group is the American Humane Association, more about which later.)

HSUS does not run any animal shelters, but does run something called the Center for Respect for Life and the Environment, headed by Michael W. Fox. He reiterated Ms. Newkirk's hatred of man when he wrote, "Man is the most dangerous, destructive, selfish, and unethical animal on earth."[18]

A similar misanthropy was expressed by Paul Watson, cofounder of Greenpeace and director of the Sea Shepherd Conservation Society: "We, the human species, have become a viral epidemic to the Earth, in truth, the AIDS of the Earth."[19]

In like manner, Sydney Singer (not be confused with Peter Singer), head of the Good Shepherd Foundation, writes, "Humans are exploiters and destroyers, self-appointed world autocrats around whom the universe seems to revolve. As a medical student, I can't afford such misanthropic feelings. But fighting them is a full-time battle."[20] Soon after writing this, Singer's misanthropy got the better of him and he dropped out of medical school. He went on to publish a book called *A Declaration of War: Killing People to Save Animals and the Environment.*[21]

To discover something very important about animal rights, read the following excerpt from *Wild Earth,* a magazine edited by David Foreman, cofounder of Earth First!:

> If you haven't given voluntary human extinction much thought before, the idea of a world with no people in it may seem strange. But, if you give it a chance, I think you might agree that the extinction of Homo sapiens would mean survival for millions, if not billions, of Earth-dwelling species.... Phasing out the human race will solve every problem on earth, social and environmental.[22]

This vision of humans as evil and animals as benevolent recalls George Orwell's classic fable of totalitarianism, *Animal Farm,* in which a group of animals overthrows the farmer and takes over his farm, chanting, "Four legs good! Two legs bad!"

Evidently, animal rightists have taken Orwell's satire seriously. In the book, "animal egalitarianism" quickly degenerates into brute elitism in which "all animals are equal, but some are more equal than others." Animal rights poses a similar threat, not only to people, but to the animals the movement purports to champion.

The warped motivation behind this warped ideology is best expressed by Ingrid Newkirk:

> I am not a morose person, but I would rather not be here. I don't have any reverence for life, only for the entities themselves. I would rather see a blank space where I am. This will sound like fruitcake stuff again but at least I wouldn't be harming anything.[23]

Such nihilism is a serious threat to all of us. Just as communism ignored economic science, animal rights ignores biologic science. In each case, the promised utopia must give way to catastrophe. But in the case of animal rights, it will not take seventy years. It will come much sooner. If these people succeed in criminalizing everything from hamburgers to leather shoes, they will have imposed total-itarianism. But by outlawing most production of food and medi-cine, they threaten to kill more people than socialism ever did.

People who are unfamiliar with animal rights must become aware of the threat it poses to our health, our safety, our freedom, and our very lives: not just to people, but to animals too; not just to our economy, but to our ecology. People who understand the threat of animal rights to their lives must go a step further and compre-hend the all-embracing threat the animal rights movement poses to all of us.

Though cloaked in the moral armor of self-righteousness, animal rights activists show contempt for the lives of ordinary people. They are engaged in an elitist war against the common man.

And they are waging their war against us all with "divide and conquer" tactics. First they go after the biomedical researchers, then the hunters and trappers, then the livestock farmers and ranchers. Eventually they will affect everyone. If we don't stand up to them now, there will be no one left to stand up for us later.

2

ANIMAL RIGHTS GROUPS
Inside the Animal Rights Movement

The world's first animal welfare group was the Royal Society for the Prevention of Cruelty to Animals (RSPCA), founded in London in 1824. In the United States, the American Society for the Prevention of Cruelty to Animals (ASPCA) was founded in 1866, the Massachusetts Society for the Prevention of Cruelty to Animals in 1868, and the American Humane Association (AHA) in 1877. These organizations established veterinary clinics and animal shelters and were concerned with improving the care of pets and livestock.

At the same time, several other groups were formed to oppose the use of animals in biomedical research. The United Kingdom saw the establishment of the National Anti-Vivisection Society in 1875, the Scottish Anti-Vivisection Society (now Animal Concerns) in 1876, and the British Union for the Abolition of Vivisection (BUAV) in 1898. In the United States, the American Anti-Vivisection Society (AAVS) was founded in 1883, the New England Antivivisection Society (NEAVS) in 1895, and the (U.S.) National Anti-Vivisection Society (NAVS) in 1929.

Smaller groups were formed to oppose hunting or promote vegetarianism, but they lacked any all-encompassing philosophy. That philosophy finally was provided in 1975 with the publication of Peter Singer's *Animal Liberation*. Some seventy animal rights groups sprang up in the following decade. Today, there may be as many as a thousand animal organizations in North America and more in Europe, although not all of them support animal rights. About 10 million Americans identify themselves as animal rights

10

advocates although, as we shall see, most do not understand what that means.

The hard core of the animal rights movement is the Animal Liberation Front (ALF). It was founded by Ronnie Lee in England in 1976, the year after Singer's book appeared. ALF evolved from an outfit called the Band of Mercy, founded by Lee and Cliff Goodman in 1972. The Band of Mercy sabotaged vehicles of hunters and destroyed guns used on bird shoots, and in 1973 committed the first two animal rights arsons, both at Hoechst Pharmaceuticals.

ALF has since spread to Germany, the Netherlands, France, Spain, Italy, Australia, Canada, Poland, and South Africa. The United States branch of ALF is believed to have been formed in 1982. It has been designated a terrorist group by the FBI.[1] ALF has no headquarters and no publicized members, but it is supported by the Animal Liberation Front Support Group of America, headed by Margo Tannenbaum, secretary of Last Chance for Animals.

Although ALF's operations are shrouded in secrecy, it receives collateral support from other groups. For example, PeTA paid more than $60,000 in fines and legal fees for self-proclaimed ALF member Roger Troen, who was convicted of burglary and theft at the University of Oregon in 1987.

Cofounded in 1980 by Alex Pacheco and Ingrid Newkirk, People for the Ethical Treatment of Animals (PeTA) is the most visible, probably the most controversial, and perhaps the most seamy public member of the animal rights movement. Although PeTA is an established organization which claims to operate openly using only peaceful methods, it has close ties to ALF. PeTA often is informed before an act of terrorism occurs, and when ALF commits an illegal act, PeTA is immediately ready to issue ALF news releases and videotapes.

PeTA claims to have 400,000 supporters. Its annual budget is approximately $10 million, although its contributions have declined recently, due, we trust, to adverse publicity from Putting People First. Nevertheless, PeTA still is in our schools, in Hollywood, and secretly in control of many other animal rights groups.

Many groups, such as the Progressive Animal Welfare Society (PAWS), In Defense of Animals (IDA), Mobilization for Animals

(MfA), the Animal Rights Foundation of Florida (ARFF), the New Jersey Animal Rights Alliance (NJARA), and Last Chance for Animals (LCA), work so closely with PeTA they could be considered as clones.

Because it is so notorious—and so dangerous—PeTA's activities will be handled separately in chapter 3.

The Fund For Animals (FFA), founded in 1967, is mostly an antihunting group with more than 200,000 members. Its president is Cleveland Amory, author of the best-sellers *The Cat Who Came for Christmas* and *The Cat and the Curmudgeon*. FFA's national director is Wayne Pacelle, who claims to be an expert on wildlife biology but whose only degree we could verify is in history. FFA agitates to ban hunting, trapping, and fishing, and challenges laws that protect hunters from harassment. FFA and PeTA work closely together.

At its Black Beauty Ranch "sanctuary," FFA was caught breeding "rescued" animals and selling the offspring for slaughter.[2] Pacelle confessed that he had been aware of the skullduggery for some time, yet FFA did not hesitate to raise a considerable sum of money from unsuspecting donors for this bogus sanctuary.

Trans-Species Unlimited (TSU) was founded by George Cave in 1981. Through harassment, it pressured Cornell University researcher Michiko Okamato into turning down a three-year $720,000 grant from the National Institute on Drug Abuse to study barbiturate addiction. TSU also sponsored antifur protests featuring game show host Bob Barker and actress Amanda Blake.

After TSU activist Fran Trutt was convicted of the attempted murder of U.S. Surgical President Leon Hirsch,[3] and after Putting People First started legal proceedings with the IRS and Postal Service to deny it nonprofit status, TSU changed its name to Animal Rights Mobilization (ARM) and soon merged with the Rocky Mountain Humane Society (RMHS). RMHS founder Robin Duxbury has been arrested for hunter harassment, and the group distributes a hunter harassment pamphlet called "Helping Hunters Kick the Habit." RMHS also promoted an unsuccessful referendum to ban fur in Aspen, Colorado, and opposes circuses and animal agriculture.

Friends of Animals (FoA) was founded in 1957 to promote

spaying and neutering. In 1969, it joined the antisealing campaign and has never looked back since. It distributes "Tips for Hunt Saboteurs" and has drafted an antitrapping bill passed in New Jersey in 1984. FoA is headed by Priscilla Feral (yes, she took the name to show her affinity with feral animals). During the seal campaign, when other groups conceded that Eskimos should be permitted to kill some seals to feed themselves, Feral complained, "We don't deal with Defenders of Wildlife or Greenpeace. I have absolute contempt for them. They're playing politics, knuckling under to the goddamn Aleuts. . . . The Aleuts don't need to eat those seals."[4]

Greenpeace is the 800-pound gorilla of the movement. It took in $169 million in 1990,[5] but its revenues have since declined by some 25 percent, due in part to the video exposé, *Survival in the High North*, by Icelandic journalist Magnus Gudmundsson (distributed by Putting People First). That documentary used computer imagery to expose "Greenpeace's intentional use of falsifications in their propaganda," including a film wherein an alleged seal hunter tormented a mother seal by dragging its pup back and forth over the ice.[6] Greenpeace's focus on marine mammals is a link between animal rights and the environmental movement. Along with the International Fund for Animal Welfare (IFAW), Greenpeace was a principal actor in the antisealing campaign.[7] Like IFAW and the Sea Shepherd Conservation Society (a Greenpeace offshoot underwritten by Cleveland Amory), its rhetoric often echoes New Age themes.

Earth First! is another link between animal rights and radical environmentalism. It was founded in 1980 and has an estimated 15,000 members. It is known for "monkey-wrenching," which involves such things as sabotaging earth-moving equipment and driving spikes into trees to damage saws. Once, at least, their spikes have caused harm, seriously injuring a millworker. Four Earth First! leaders were convicted of conspiracy to sabotage a nuclear power plant. Earth First! has no known list of its membership and reports no dues.

Dave Foreman, cofounder of Earth First!, believes humans have no special claim to the earth's resources. "A Grizzly Bear snuffling along Pelican Creek in Yellowstone National Park with her two cubs has just as much right to life as any human has, and is far more important ecologically," he says.[8]

Earth First! has claimed joint responsibility with ALF for arsons at meat plants and has participated in antifur protests by TSU. *Earth First! Journal* publishes many articles by ALF, including a series by Rodney Coronado, an indicted fugitive and a suspect in several arsons. One purported Earth First! offshoot is the Voluntary Human Extinction Movement (VHEMT).

Many front groups are set up and funded by the larger animal rights organizations to exploit people who use animals in one fashion by attacking others who use animals differently.[9] For example, the Medical Research Modernization Committee (MRMC) and Physicians Committee for Responsible Medicine (PCRM), which is funded by PeTA, can recruit hunters and farmers to attack researchers; the Committee to Abolish Sport Hunting (CASH) can recruit researchers and farmers to attack hunters; and groups like the Farm Animal Reform Movement (FARM) and Beyond Beef Coalition (BBC) can recruit researchers and hunters to attack farmers. This "divide and conquer" strategy permits the movement to use its opponents to destroy each other.

On the fringe are groups like the Good Shepherd Foundation and its offshoots, the All Beings Are Created Equal Church (ABACE) and the Liberators, an alleged group that, according to its spokesman "Screaming Wolf," is even more violent than ALF.

New Age groups like the Humane Vegetarian Church and Buddhists for Animal Rights give the movement an exotic air. Then there are groups such as Feminists for Animal Rights, the Women's Wilderness Warriors, and something called Eco-Dykes, which protests gay rodeos.

Back here on earth, the old mainline animal welfare organizations are exhibiting an alarming tendency to become more militant, in some cases, because they see that animal rights is where the money is. But in other cases, animal rights groups have taken over the boards of animal welfare groups to get at their endowments, as ALF did to BUAV and PeTA did to NEAVS.

Many local humane societies have become active animal rights organizations. Some now oppose dog breeding, object to the use of animals for medical research, and want to do away with hunting, trapping, and dog racing. Says PeTA's Ingrid Newkirk, "Humane societies all over the country are adopting the animal rights philosophy [and are] becoming vegetarian."[10]

On a larger scale, the ASPCA, which was formed to promote animal welfare, has gradually shifted toward adopting the animal rights agenda. ASPCA President John Kullberg proclaims, "The major success of this decade [the 1980s] has been the reapplication of the concept of rights in the human population to nonhuman species."[11]

ASPCA now encourages vegetarianism, the banning of fur, and the eventual end to all animal research, not just "cruel" animal research. ASPCA lawyers successfully championed the cause of biology students who were opposed to dissecting frogs. Kullberg urges these students to "get in touch with us, and we'll take on a lawsuit."[12]

ASPCA publications call upon parents to stop reading "Little Red Riding Hood" and "Three Blind Mice" to their children because these stories portray animals in a derogatory way. The publications also tell children to stop singing "Old MacDonald Had a Farm" because it depicts farm animals as happy.

The Humane Society of the United States (HSUS), for its part, currently serves as a front to legitimatize the animal rights movement to pet owners.[13] HSUS split off from AHA in 1954. In 1980, it adopted the animal rights line that "there is no rational basis for maintaining a moral distinction between the treatment of humans and other animals."[14] It grew from 65,000 supporters that year to over a million by 1990. It now takes in close to $20 million a year.[15]

Many people make contributions to HSUS thinking the organization provides money for animal shelters. In fact, HSUS does not run a single shelter. It benefits from the confusing similarity of its name with that of the much older AHA, of which many local shelters are members. AHA was originally called the American Humane Society. But even AHA has now started to move from being an animal welfare organization to promoting certain aspects of the animal rights agenda.

HSUS devotes its time to lobbying against hunting, fur, and research, and to supporting vegetarianism. It also campaigns against the breeding of pets. Officially, HSUS claims to accept the need for the use of animals in medical experiments. But in its fund-raising literature, it attacks biomedical research as "absolutely horrifying"[16] and campaigns to ban the use of unwanted pound animals in biomedical research.

Animal rights is one very big money-making machine. It's hard to estimate the exact income of the animal rights movement because often the line between animal welfare groups and animal rights organizations is blurred. But the reliable estimates we have seen of the income of all animal rights organizations vary between $60 million and $200 million annually. One estimate places it as high as $300 million.[17]

Well-meaning contributors who think that their animal rights donations are used for animals are either misinformed or naive about where the money goes. According to a 1990 survey of thirty-three top animal advocacy groups, over 90 percent of the money raised annually by these groups was spent sending out requests to raise more money. Almost nothing was spent directly for the benefit of animals.[18]

What doesn't get spent on fund-raising often ends up lining the pockets of the groups' leaders. In 1988, columnist Jack Anderson reported that HSUS President John Hoyt and Treasurer Paul Irwin were receiving even more compensation for their work than their own board members knew about.[19] Anderson discovered that HSUS bought Hoyt's $310,000 home for him in Maryland and allowed Irwin to write himself $85,000 in checks for a real estate venture, which the board renamed a "loan." Hoyt's and Irwin's salaries and benefits at the time amounted to more than $139,000 and $114,000 respectively. That kind of money could have bought a whole lot of dog food, but then HSUS doesn't run any animal shelters.[20]

Anderson's followup article in 1991 quoted California's attorney general, who wrote to HSUS that the charity had "engaged in a course of conduct" that "violated" the charity trust laws of California.

How do animal rights groups manage to raise all this money?

Part of the explanation is their misleading but lucrative direct mail appeals, labeled by the Direct Marketing Archive as "the new pornography."[21] But look also at the socioeconomic composition of the people they manipulate.

The typical animal rights activist is a white woman making about $30,000 a year. She is most likely a schoolteacher, nurse, or government worker. She usually has a college degree or even an advanced degree, is in her thirties or forties, and lives in a city. She has five pets but no children.

This portrait of animal rights activists has been drawn from two separate studies by Utah State University and Oregon State University researchers. Rebecca Richards and Richard Krannich, the Utah State researchers, conducted a random sample survey of subscribers to *Animals' Agenda*, an animal rights publication. The survey was based on 853 responses, or 84 percent of the total mailed, and was funded by an animal rights foundation.[22] Wes Jamison and William Lunch, the Oregon State researchers, led a team interviewing 412 animal activists attending an animal rights march on Washington on June 9 and 10, 1990.[23] The numbers the two different researchers came up with are remarkably similar.

Looking at the numbers, you can see the major advantage of animal rights organizations. Although the protest marchers are generally less well off, both groups have enough high earners to ensure the movement a continuing hefty financial response to their appeals for money. Animal rights groups can draw on the support of women who do not have to devote their energies to children. And they can use the knowledge and skills of these professional workers to mobilize political support—whether for demonstrations or lobbying.

But according to the Jamison-Lunch survey, most people who call themselves animal rights activists do not really know the full agenda they are supporting. Only 55 percent oppose all use of animals in research, and fully 87 percent approve keeping pets. Ironically, these people are being exploited by a movement that regards *them* as exploiters.

Animal rights activists regard themselves as "ultraliberal." When asked to rate themselves ideologically on a scale from 1 to 9, where 1

A PORTRAIT OF ANIMAL RIGHTS ACTIVISTS

	Animals' Agenda Subscribers[a]	Protest Marchers[b]
SEX		
Male	21.7	31.6
Female	78.3	68.4
AGE		
29 and under	23.2	41.9
30 to 49	56.6	48.0
50 and over	20.0	6.4
RACE		
White	96.9	92.9
Nonwhite	3.1	7.1
EDUCATION		
High school diploma, GED or less	17.9	12.3
Bachelor's degree or some college	48.4	40.2
Some graduate school	NA	7.1
Masters or professional degree	33.3	18.7
INCOME		
$19,999 or less	18.4	19.0
$20,000 to $49,999	42.5	46.1
$50,000 or more	38.9	18.7
RESIDENCE		
Urban	73.4	88.2
Rural	26.6	NA
OCCUPATION		
Those citing "professional" or executive status	46.0	44.0

[a] Richards-Krannich survey
[b] Jamison-Lunch survey

is conservative and 9 liberal, a whopping 69 percent placed themselves on the liberal side from 6 through 9, while only 10 percent placed themselves on the conservative side from 1 to 4. Sixteen percent rated themselves a moderate 5; 10 percent gave themselves the most liberal 9; but none gave the most conservative 1.[24]

The movement's bias is not just left-wing; it is against productive people and for political agitation. When asked to rate their approval or disapproval of various groups on a scale of zero to 100, where zero is the most negative and 100 the most positive, animal rightists rated feminists 76 percent, environmentalists 97 percent, and, not surprisingly, animal rights activists 100 percent. In contrast, they rated farmers a dismal 25 percent, and scientists and businessmen only 21 and 20 percent respectively, even lower than politicians (23 percent!).

Most activists share a bias against Western civilization and its Judeo-Christian foundations. Eighty-seven percent agreed with the statement: "The main cause of animal exploitation is the world view that humanity has dominion over the animals." A 52 percent majority said, "Science does more harm than good," with only 26 percent disagreeing, and 22 percent with no opinion. At the March on Washington, they promoted this Luddite message, without a hint of irony, through a sound system powered by electricity from internal-combustion engines in gas-burning generators.

Despite the left-wing slant of the movement, its political clout is surprisingly bipartisan. But most of the leading politicians working with the animal rights movement are liberal Democrats. Senator Barbara Boxer of California was a major sponsor of antimedical research legislation when she was a member of the House, and will undoubtedly continue now that she has moved up to the Senate. Nevada Congressman Jim Bilbray was awarded a medal of honor by PeTA in 1993 and worked hard to defeat legislation that created stiff new federal penalties for animal rights-related break-ins, bombings, and other conspiracies. With the help of Putting People First, that bill passed over Bilbray's opposition.

The U.S. House of Representatives is full of Democratic animal rights fellow travelers. Possibly the craftiest is Charlie Rose of North Carolina, who reportedly maneuvered himself into the chairmanship of a roadblock Agriculture Subcommittee. He tried to use his chairmanship to block the antiterrorist legislation previously mentioned.

Other Democratic congressmen we are always fighting include Tom Lantos, who chairs the Hill's animal rights caucus (Congressional Friends of Animals), and Gerry Studds, now chairman of the House Fisheries Committee. Studds sponsored a successful bill in 1992 that will virtually shut down the U.S. tuna industry by banning tuna fishing involving dolphins instead of requiring stringent precautions to guard against killing dolphins.

But some Republicans are animal rightists, too. Senate Minority Leader Bob Dole of Kansas often supports animal rights causes—except, of course, those pertaining to cattle, a major business in Kansas. Senator Robert Smith of New Hampshire was a founder of the Congressional Friends of Animals. Bob Dornan of California, one of the most conservative House members, is an animal rights advocate—he cosponsored legislation banning the use of animals in testing cosmetics and received a PeTA award. And Manhattan Congressman Bill Green promoted legislation that would have shut down over 90 million acres of federal land to hunting, fishing, and trapping. Putting People First stymied that bill, and in 1992 helped defeat Congressman Green too.

Although he's not an elected official, a conservative political figure who, surprisingly, is on the other side is G. Gordon Liddy, author of *Will* and a key figure in the 1972 Watergate uproar. When I went on Liddy's radio show, he and PeTA's Ingrid Newkirk greeted each other with hugs and kisses and lots of warm words.

With allies in both political parties and across the ideological spectrum, the animal rights movement has been able to score some great successes, regardless of which party controls the White House or Capitol Hill. Those successes include statutes and regulations that have caused enormous problems and financial damage to the targets of animal rights advocates.

Animal rights groups, through fraudulent claims, are stealing money from well-meaning animal lovers. They are immersed in illegality through misuse of funds for personal gain. And they are brainwashing children. (For a list of animal rights groups, see appendix 2.)

They have an agenda that is doing terrible damage to our future. They are not fighting for animals. They are fighting against medical research and the education of future scientists who could make contributions to curing some of the most baffling, debilitating, and painful diseases known to man.

If they get their way, they will drive every person from any job that involves the use of animals, whether it is a cook in a fast-food restaurant, a zoologist caring for an animal at a wildlife refuge, a rancher raising cattle, or a pest-control employee treating an infestation of bugs. And as these pages will show, they hope to take seeing-eye dogs away from the blind.

They are aided by powerful allies in politics and society, and by their slick public relations that put them on the side of animals. But most of all, they are sustained by the contributions they receive from a public that is uninformed about their true agenda.

3

THE SPECIAL CASE OF PeTA
"A Rat Is a Pig Is a Dog Is a Boy"

PeTA is the most infamous of the animal rights organizations. Its success in fund-raising and with Hollywood celebrities has given it a cachet that is the envy of other groups. It has come a long way since Alex Pacheco, then unemployed, and Ingrid Newkirk, a British-born animal control officer for the District of Columbia, founded the group in July 1980. Pacheco now is chairman and Newkirk national director of PeTA.

As of this writing PeTA has a paid staff of more than eighty people and claims to have 400,000 members, but actually has only three. In 1987, PeTA's three-member board of directors (Newkirk, Pacheco, and Kim Stallwood) voted themselves the only "members" of the organization.[1]

By amending the Articles of Incorporation, these three were able to convert their "members" into customer/contributors and themselves into a self-perpetuating multimillion-dollar partnership. They thereby circumvented the law in Delaware (where PeTA was incorporated) that grants "members" a right to vote for the board, remove directors for cause, and examine the corporate books.

What does PeTA have to hide? The group reported an annual budget of $10.5 million in 1991, with more than $9 million coming from contributions and most of the rest from the sale of PeTA merchandise. Thanks in part, we believe, to Putting People First, PeTA's 1992 budget fell to $8.5 million.

That's still enough money to save an awful lot of animals—especially since it's all tax-exempt. But PeTA does not use one single cent of its money to purchase wildlife habitat, find homes for strays, spay and neuter pets, or research alternative biomedical or wildlife management techniques. PeTA, of course, claims to protect animals from suffering and abuse. But to PeTA, that means attacking medical researchers, hunters, trappers, farmers, furriers, meat companies, restaurants, circuses, zoos, rodeos, and pet shops.

PeTA is an animal "rights" or animal "liberation" group. It bears no similarity to "humane" or "animal welfare" organizations, with which PeTA is apt to be confused. Animal welfare organizations seek the humane treatment of animals. Animal rights groups, in contrast, believe that humane treatment is irrelevant: all use of animals by people, no matter how humane or necessary, should be banned.

To PeTA, pet ownership is the moral equivalent of slavery. (See chapter 6.) Laboratory research using animals is an abomination, even to save human lives. The organization is against eating meat, drinking milk, hunting, and fishing.

To top PeTA officials, those who do not share their ideology— animal trainers, hunters, fishermen, cattlemen, grocers, and indeed all nonvegetarians—are the moral equivalent of cannibals and slaveowners and must be dealt with accordingly. Personal defamation is a minor retribution for such crimes.

PeTA exploded from a loose group of one or two dozen radicals into a multimillion-dollar concern as a result of its 1981 attack on Dr. Edward Taub. Dr. Taub is a behavioral scientist of national standing, whose work is largely devoted to rehabilitating stroke and head injury victims.[2] He has paid particular attention to "deafferentation"—what occurs when a stroke cuts off all sensation in a body part. The limb affected is often initially paralyzed, and generally atrophies and becomes useless.

Taub's work with macaque monkeys demonstrated that this need not be the case. If a monkey's arm or leg was made deafferented by surgery, the actual paralysis was temporary—the monkey could be trained to use it. To be sure, being forced to eat and move with a supposedly useless arm was burdensome to the monkeys; but being disabled is still more burdensome to the 25,000 American stroke victims with deafferentation injuries.

Shortly after PeTA's establishment, Alex Pacheco infiltrated Dr. Taub's laboratory in Silver Spring, Maryland, posing as a student. Pacheco obtained funding and technical help, such as walkie-talkies, from the Fund for Animals. An accomplice acted as look-out while Pacheco entered the lab to copy Dr. Taub's papers and take pictures.

In August 1981, Taub went on vacation and left the monkeys in the care of assistants friendly to Pacheco. Pacheco's new friends failed to clean the cages or feed the animals on certain days, the very days Pacheco happened to take activists—including members of the Humane Society of the United States—on unauthorized night-time tours of the lab.[3]

Pacheco took his findings to local law enforcement, which seized the monkeys on September 11, 1981, while PeTA distributed a press release accusing Dr. Taub of 119 violations of the Animal Welfare Act.

PeTA promptly ran a large fund-raising ad, and began a direct-mail campaign that would eventually reach between 10 and 20 million people—source of funding unknown—based on the story, using photographs stolen from Dr. Taub. Readers were exhorted to send money to defray legal costs although the only action pending was brought by the government, which does not accept contributions for prosecutions (other than your involuntary tax dollars).

The money raised by PeTA was in fact used to retain a professional fund-raiser from California, later replaced by Gary Thorud, former head of the Washington office of CARE.

Prior to trial, the monkeys (although evidence in custody of the court) were housed at a PeTA member's residence. When the court ordered them returned to Dr. Taub, the monkeys mysteriously vanished.

The prosecuting attorney, Roger Galvin (who shortly thereafter resigned to help found the Animal Legal Defense Fund), brought a seventeen-count indictment against Taub. Eleven of the seventeen counts were dismissed at trial; five of the remaining six ended in acquittal; the last was overturned and dismissed on appeal.[4]

If PeTA were interested in preventing abuse rather than raising money, Taub's final acquittal should have ended the fund-raising. But a full decade after Taub's victory, PeTA was fund-raising off its acts by marketing a $15 videotape, "The Silver Spring Monkeys," which smeared Taub as thoroughly as if he had been convicted.

The Silver Spring monkeys, observed the *Washington Post*, "turned Alex Pacheco into a public figure and helped to make PeTA the largest, most powerful—and most feared—animal-rights group in America."[5]

In due course, some of the monkeys began to suffer from old age, but PeTA's legal maneuvers delayed euthanasia in order to use them to raise more money. When the monkeys were finally put out of their misery, researchers performed an autopsy and made an important medical discovery: a significantly larger portion of each monkey's brain than had previously been thought possible had "rewired" itself to process nerve signals that had been "disconnected" twelve years before.[6]

While PeTA was still agitating about cruelty to monkeys, a whistleblower from within the organization told the press that PeTA had secretly killed more than thirty healthy "rescued" rabbits and roosters at its "sanctuary," the Aspin Hill pet cemetery near Washington, D.C.[7]

When challenged, Pacheco and Newkirk claimed that their killings did not violate animal rights. U.S. Congressman Vin Weber, founder of the Congressional Animal Welfare Caucus, was skeptical. "If mercy killing is truly consistent with the animal rights philosophy, why the fanatical opposition to the killing of the Silver Spring monkeys for the very same reason?" asked Weber. "Could it be that the monkeys are too valuable a fund-raising tool for PeTA to give up?"[8]

Indeed, PeTA had used the "rescue" of the rabbits from a local school to urge supporters to make "a special contribution." *PeTA Kids* magazine assured children that Aspin Hill was "a special place where animals can live without fear of people hurting or killing them."[9]

What happened to all the money raised for Aspin Hill? PeTA's former chief accountant, Sam Alston, has testified under oath that

PeTA Executive Director Kim Stallwood "and his male friend at the [Aspin Hill] cemetery, Gary Bevestock" achieved "personal financial gain" by "shorting" Aspin Hill funds.[10]

PeTA imported Kim Stallwood from England in 1986. According to PeTA's own employees, Stallwood boasted of his connections with Animal Liberation Front (ALF) terrorists. "He had been a member of ALF and came over to train Alex and Ingrid in America, [and] was very proud of that relationship," testified Gary Thorud.[11]

Shortly after Stallwood's arrival in the United States, PeTA began leveraging its money to take over wealthy older groups, much as ALF had taken over the British Union to Abolish Vivisection (BUAV) when Stallwood was there. Like a ruthless Wall Street raider, PeTA took over the New England Anti-Vivisection Society, with its $8 million endowment. As the *Boston Globe* reported:

> The wife of Gary Francione, a PETA executive and a Pennsylvania attorney, walked into the Anti-Vivisection Society's Boston headquarters a few months ago and purchased 300 voting memberships for $3,000 in cash. . . .
>
> A surge of several hundred applications for voting membership arrived at the headquarters in bulk. . . .
>
> PETA set up the Action Campaign Fund to subsidize or pay full airfare to Boston for an unspecified number of voting activists. . . . [O]ne activist from a Midwestern state . . . described how more than two dozen tickets had already been reserved with PETA's permission.[12]

A PeTA slate also captured the Toronto Humane Society, whose funds have since apparently been used to support animal-rights terrorists. Again, from the *Boston Globe*:

> A PETA consultant won control of the Toronto Humane Society, endowed with $14 million, last fall through a proxy fight. One of her employees recently was arrested for possession of explosives and weapons, and vandalizing a restaurant that served chicken. . . .[13]

Soon after PeTA's establishment, animal rights terrorism surged in the United States. Alex Pacheco called animal rights arson, burglary, and destruction of property "acceptable crimes." Immediately prior to founding PeTA, Pacheco, by his own admission, gained experience in animal rights violence. He took passage aboard the *Sea Shepherd*, a ship financed by Cleveland Amory, the founder of Fund For Animals. The ship rammed and nearly sank a whaler on the high seas. Its crew was arrested and imprisoned.

Upon his release, Pacheco joined the Hunt Saboteurs Association, a British group specializing in vandalizing hunters' vehicles— slashing tires and smashing windshields.[14]

The *Washington Post* reported as early as 1983 that PeTA's executive director Ingrid Newkirk "has endorsed—and on occasion served as intermediary for—a clandestine group called the Animal Liberation Front."[15]

Newkirk gave further insight into PeTA's terrorist sympathies in an interview in 1985:

CP [*City Paper* Interviewer]: These groups also destroy and have according to their own assertions destroyed millions of dollars worth of equipment. Do you agree with those tactics?

IN [Ingrid Newkirk]: ... We don't choose to do those tactics here. I certainly more firmly disagree with the people who destroy and mutilate living things. ...

CP: Destroying property is violating a human right, isn't it?

IN: Is it the human's right to torture others? We don't believe so. Human beings don't have any rights to torture, to harm, and to destroy. No, you don't own those animals.

CP: Have you collaborated with them at all in planning some of the raids in which they destroy property?

IN: If we had we wouldn't say so. We don't discuss anything to do with that. We would never place them in jeopardy.[16]

But a PeTA Factsheet entitled "The Animal Liberation Front: The Army of the Kind," suggests just such collaboration:

The Animal Liberation Front's activities comprise an important part of today's animal protection movement ... Without ALF break-ins ... many more animals would have suffered. ...[17]

As Pacheco himself has admitted, PeTA serves as a "PR firm for ALF, in a sense."[18] That means PeTA is a "PR firm" for terror. The FBI and Scotland Yard have formally classified ALF as a terrorist organization. The FBI considers ALF responsible for more than 270 criminal attacks, including several classified as domestic terrorism. Yet ALF receives full-page ads in PeTA's journal. The ads feature the "ALF Credo," which includes a commitment "to economically sabotage the industries of animal exploitation."[19] (For a partial list of animal rights extremist incidents, see appendix 3.)

PeTA publishes a pamphlet, "Activism and the Law," which suggests that while the decision to undertake "illegal actions" may be unpopular, "no struggle against exploitation has been won without them."[20]

PeTA ends its pamphlet with a "Sample Case" in which a couple is stopped "in the vicinity of the burglary of a primate research center." PeTA's activists are given this hypothesis:

> As he reaches into a coat pocket to pull out a wallet, one of the officers spins him around, pats down his clothing, and pulls out the sole contents of the other pocket: a map of the research center with the surveillance camera and burglar alarm locations clearly marked. The officers order Brown to open his pack. He refuses to do so, stating that the pack contains only camping gear. The officers arrest Brown, searching his pack and discover burglary tools and stolen research files.[21]

Activists then are asked to think out the legal situation when the couple is brought to trial. This is surely one of the few cases in which a tax-exempt organization provides written legal counsel prior to the commission of a crime.

PeTA and ALF work in a lucrative partnership, profiting from terror. In a typical attack in 1989, ALF burglars broke into and entered the laboratories of Dr. John Orem at Texas Tech University and Health Sciences Center. Dr. Orem had been investigating Sudden Infant Death Syndrome (or "crib death"), a major cause of death in the very young. Animals were taken, as were his personal records, walls were spray-painted, and over $50,000 in equipment was destroyed. Within days, PeTA held a press conference claiming that Dr. Orem had "turned cats into an appliance you could plug into a wall."[22]

Typically, PeTA took advantage of ALF's felonious conduct to raise funds.

When PeTA filed a formal complaint against Dr. Orem alleging violations of Public Health Service (PHS) policy in September 1989, that was big news. But in March 1990, the Office of Protection from Research Risks (OPRR), the branch of the NIH responsible for investigating allegations of research animal abuse, concluded "that there has been no substantive evidence" to support complaints against the center and Orem. It stated firmly, "OPRR has no reason to consider further action on these allegations and considers this matter closed."[23]

Yet PeTA continued to exploit the Orem hoax. Members were urged to write Orem's home address, to "help sponsor one of our new billboards" (displaying a picture of a cat labeled "Texas Tech Killed This Cat"), or to purchase an $18 video from PeTA. PeTA is still selling the video, described as "an exposé of John Orem's ride on the federal grant gravy train and the story of five cats slated for death in his laboratory. . . ."[24]

The year after Taub's acquittal, ALF burglarized laboratories at the University of Pennsylvania, which were developing therapies for serious head injuries. In recent animal testing, therapies have been developed that have counteracted the effects of stroke or trauma and greatly limited the damage.

The break-in at the University of Pennsylvania involved theft of six years of research data, as well as extensive vandalism of computers and medical equipment. Another involved the theft of animals being used in research on arthritis and Sudden Infant Death Syndrome. Shortly thereafter, PeTA distributed ALF press releases attacking the research and distributed selected portions of the stolen materials intending to harm the reputation of the researchers. According to one news account:

> The incident gained national press attention, culminating in an appearance on the Phil Donahue Show by People for the Ethical Treatment of Animals' co-founder Ingrid Newkirk. . . . The University remained the center of controversy when the California-based Animal Legal Defense Fund threatened to file suit. . . .[25]

The close partnership between PeTA and the Animal Legal Defense Fund (ALDF) is noteworthy. ALDF's annual report notes that it was involved in defense of activists facing "criminal charges arising from the break-in at the University of Pennsylvania Head Injury Laboratory and the showing of the videotape. . . . After the receipt of 60 hours of head injury videotapes by PeTA, ALDF attorneys began a series of FOIA [Freedom of Information Act] requests. . . ." The report goes on to note ALDF's success in preventing grand jury testimony relating to the break-in, and in overseeing "the highly successful National Institutes of Health sit-in which is credited with forcing the final closing of the head injury laboratory. . . ."[26]

But one brave University of Pennsylvania veterinarian, Dr. Adrian Morrison, who did not work at the Head Injury Lab, spoke out in defense of its work as well as of Drs. Taub and Orem. This lone voice was too much for the "humanitarians." ALF retaliated by burglarizing Dr. Morrison's office, stealing his personal correspondence, and vandalizing the room. According to one account:

> Morrison's office was broken into Jan. 14 [1990]. The militant Animal Liberation Front took credit. Yesterday, PETA released what it said was a "preliminary examination" of copies of documents taken in the break-in. The review concluded that Morrison had written letters supporting other researchers and that he planned to oppose certain "animal protective legislation."[27]

PeTA made it clear that Dr. Morrison was attacked because he had dared to speak freely. PeTA was now attacking the First Amendment. The *Village Voice* printed Ingrid Newkirk's chilling statement applauding the attack:

> PETA intends to use Morrison as an example to persuade other vivisectors, who were heartened by his strong stand on animal research, that it doesn't pay off. . . . Now the spotlight is on him, and what happens next will deter others who might want to follow in his footsteps.[28]

What happened next? PeTA sent copies of the *Village Voice* story to all of Morrison's neighbors, with a note beginning: "Please see the enclosed *Village Voice* cover story involving your neighbor Adrian Morrison, who lives at [address deleted for this book]," and quoting from some of the stolen correspondence. A few months later, PeTA proudly informed its members of its treatment of a man who dared to speak out:

> Tired out from the ALF raid on his Penn lab, Adrian Morrison got a grant to spend a month in Italy this summer visiting fellow cat-electrode implanter Pier Permeggani. . . . [T]he real highlight of Morrison's trip was being discovered, exposed, and picketed by Animal Amnesty, a PETA contact group. Thanks to the activists, there really is no rest for the wicked![29]

Substantial money is raised through such attacks, but with little accountability. When ALF member Roger Troen was convicted of burglary and arson at the University of Oregon, in which $36,000 in damage was inflicted,[30] PeTA paid Troen's $27,000 legal fees and his $34,900 fine. Gary Thorud testified under oath that "we were illegally funding this individual with money solicited for other causes, and Ingrid was using that money, bragging to the staff that she had spent $25,000 on the case."[31]

Similarly, when Fran Trutt was convicted of the attempted murder of Leon Hirsch, president of U.S. Surgical Corporation, PeTA contributed $7,500 to her defense.

PeTA funds are used not only to support terrorism, but reportedly to line the pockets of its leaders. PeTA's former chief accountant, Sam Alston, testified under oath that, during his tenure, Alex Pacheco was sending PeTA donations "down to an organization in Mexico, and after questioning I found out that someone by the name of Alex Pacheco was president [of that organization], but I cannot say for sure if it was Alex Pacheco who is the chairperson of PeTA. . . ."[32]

As I write this book, PeTA is under investigation by federal grand juries in Michigan, Oregon, Washington, Utah, and Louisiana. Ingrid Newkirk and Alex Pacheco have been subpoenaed to provide fingerprints and handwriting samples to the FBI. They are under investigation for conspiracy, arson, terrorism, and racketeering.

According to *U.S. News and World Report,* which reported the PeTA investigations, conviction of violation of the Racketeer Influenced and Corrupt Organizations Act (RICO) carries penalties of up to twenty-five years in prison, millions of dollars in fines, and forfeiture of assets.[33]

Yet PeTA is using this investigation as yet another fund-raising opportunity, begging its supporters for "your most generous gift ever" for its "Activists' Defense Fund."[34]

Animal lovers who send money to PeTA may inadvertently be funding lies, terrorism, and a lavish lifestyle for the group's leaders. They are certainly not helping animals. Political personalities in Washington and celebrities of stage and screen in New York and Hollywood who identify with PeTA should stop posturing and wake up to reality.

Animals deserve better than groups like PeTA.

PART TWO

PEOPLE AND ANIMALS: ANIMAL RIGHTS LIES ABOUT ANIMAL WELFARE AND CONSERVATION

WHO BELEIVES IN SPARING
ANIMALS TORTURE IN LABS?
SIGN HERE OK ANYWHERE ELSE

1. D.T.

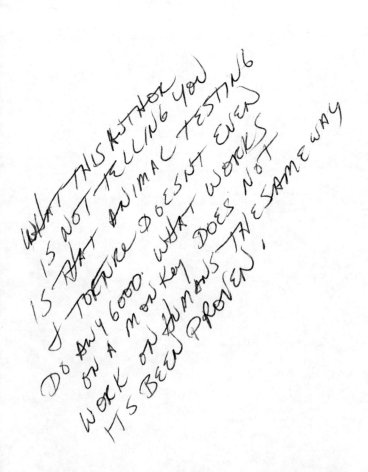

WHAT THIS AUTHOR
IS NOT TELLING YOU
IS THAT ANIMAL TESTING
& TORTURE DOESN'T EVEN
DO ANY GOOD. WHAT WORKS
ON A MONKEY DOES NOT
WORK ON HUMANS THE SAME WAY
ITS BEEN PROVEN.

4

ANIMALS IN SCIENCE
Spare the Rat and Kill the Child

[handwritten annotation: I WOULD NOT HAVE AN ANIMAL DIE TO SPARE MY LIFE AND WHAT'S WRONG WITH THAT? THAT'S CALLED COMPASSION THIS AUTHOR HAS NONE]

Your child is dying. Doctors have run out of all medical options except one—to use an animal's organ in an experimental transplant operation. Do you tell the doctors to proceed? Or do you say, as Fund For Animals founder Cleveland Amory said in a 1987 interview, "I would not knowingly have an animal hurt for me, or my children, or anything else"?[1]

For most of us, it is no contest. We value the life of any human being—let alone that of a loved one—more than that of a dog, pig, or baboon. And yet, if animal rights activists have their way, your child would die so the animal could live.

In June 1992, a thirty-five-year-old man became the world's first recipient of a transplanted baboon liver.[2] After the operation was performed at the University of Pittsburgh Medical Center, angry animal rights protesters screamed, "There are no lesser creatures" and "Animals are not expendable."

Suzanne E. Roy, public affairs director of In Defense of Animals, wrote the *New York Times* to condemn animal-human transplants, along with genetic engineering techniques that use animal cells to produce cancer-fighting monoclonal antibodies: "The animal kingdom will become nothing more than spare parts supply houses and drug-producing factories for humankind."[3]

But if we're already raising animals for chopped liver, why shouldn't a dying man use the liver whole? Man has always raised animals to enhance the quality of life; now we can raise them to save lives.

The medical profession rallied around the physicians in Pittsburgh. Jeffrey A. Romoff, president of the medical center, maintained that the medical center's obligation was to help patients.

In this case, using a baboon's liver was the last chance to save this human life. The man was dying from recurring infections of the hepatitis B virus, which attacks the liver. Even if a human liver had been available for a transplant, there was an 85 percent chance the virus would have damaged it as well and thereby killed the patient. But since baboons seem not to be affected by hepatitis B, the animal's liver could relieve the man of his viral symptoms, according to Dr. Thomas Starzl, director of the Transplantation Institute at the medical center.[4]

The patient lived for seventy-one days and then died from a brain hemorrhage unrelated to the liver transplant. Although this procedure is still in the experimental stage, the prospects of success were sufficiently encouraging for the doctors to plan repeating the medical procedure with new patients.

If future operations involving transplantation across species—or xenografts, as they are called—are successful, the implications are profound. Worldwide an estimated 250,000 people die of liver cancer annually, and more than 200 million people are chronically infected with the hepatitis B virus. Hepatitis in its different forms is one of the most common infectious human diseases. The transplant operation in Pittsburgh gave new hope to the victims of this dreaded disease, many of whom now face an early death.

In 1992, an estimated 27,391 people were on waiting lists for organ transplants in the United States, according to the United Network for Organ Sharing in Richmond, Virginia.[5] Because of the shortage of human organs, many will die. The prospect that animal organs could be used offers hope.

Animal rightists demand that people like the patient in Pittsburgh pay a high price for the activists' ideals—namely, death. But do they practice what they preach?

Their record is poor. When it comes to using medicines derived from animal research, they have not let their principles stand in their way. When Putting People First invited these animal rightists to authorize their doctors not to use medication or surgical techniques derived from animals when their own health was in jeopardy, not a single activist came forward.

THE PLEDGE THAT ANIMAL RIGHTISTS REFUSE TO TAKE

MEDICAL ALERT

I believe that animals should not be used in scientific or medical research.

If I am unable to speak for myself in a medical emergency, do NOT treat me using any medical or surgical device, procedure, or drug which was developed using animals as experimental subjects.

DATE   SIGNATURE

Animal rightists could take a lesson in consistency from evangelist Billy Graham. He provoked a lot of controversy for his opposition to abortion, but he garnered respect even from opponents when he was diagnosed with Alzheimer's disease and refused experimental fetal tissue injections to treat it.

By contrast, consider the animal rightists' opposition to insulin for diabetes, perhaps the greatest success in the history of animal research. Diabetes mellitus is the leading cause of blindness, kidney failure, and amputations, as well as increasing the risk of heart disease and stroke. Insulin, a by-product of meat-packing industries, is isolated from the pancreas of animals, and has saved countless lives by controlling diabetes. The American Diabetes Association sponsors a "Kiss-a-Pig" contest to say "thanks" to pigs and other animals for saving the lives of millions of people. Fund For Animals callously attacks the contest as a celebration of "animal exploitation."

Yet PeTA's director of research and investigations, Mary Beth Sweetland has admitted, "I'm an insulin-dependent diabetic. Twice a day I take synthetically manufactured insulin that still contains some animal products—and I have no qualms about it." Sweetland adds, "I don't see myself as a hypocrite. I need my life to fight for the rights of animals."[6] She argues that she is permitted to exploit animals because she is not a "speciesist."

Sweetland had her son vaccinated when he was young, but that was before she became an animal rights believer. In the same story in *Glamour* she said, "I was recently encouraged to give him a tetanus-diphtheria booster shot, and I turned it down."

Of course, should the child fall victim to tetanus or diphtheria, he could proclaim his support for animal rights and thereby become worthy of a life-saving vaccine.

In their zeal to stop animal research, animal rightists even deny that vaccines work.[7] They claim the reason a disease dies out is either because everyone has been infected who is going to get the disease, or else those not infected have developed some "natural system" of immunity to the illness. They often cite polio as an example.

There were 58,000 cases of polio in the United States in 1952. By 1984, the entire country had four cases of polio. This miracle happened thanks to vaccines developed by two teams of scientists using animals.

Sadly, polio has since been reintroduced, in part because some immigrants coming into the United States have not been vaccinated, and in part because various U.S. citizens have been unable or unwilling to have their children vaccinated—some because of fraudulent animal rights arguments.

The tragedy of refusing immunization is not limited to polio. Measles had been nearly eradicated in the 1980s. But once again, because parents have failed to have their children vaccinated, doctors are reporting an increase in measles among children.

Vaccination is not perfect, and in rare cases causes bad side effects. But it's guaranteed that refusing to take vaccines will have catastrophic health consequences, such as the dramatic recent rise of polio, measles, typhoid, smallpox, and whooping cough.

Animal rights activists claim that people and animals are physiologically too different for animal models to work. In fact, more than

250 diseases are common to both humans and animals, and many treatments are the same in both veterinary and human medicine, such as insulin and human polio vaccines.

The animal rights obsession with medical research distorts perspective by exaggerating the number of animals used in science. Here are some facts: worldwide, 97.5 percent of animals are used for food or fiber, and another 2.1 percent are pets, according to Dr. Arthur Guyton. Research, testing, and education account for only 0.4 percent of animals used.[8]

In the United States, Guyton adds, 5 billion animals are used for all purposes every year. Of this amount, 100 million (2 percent) are pets, while 22 million (less than one-half of 1 percent) are used in science. Of these, 90 to 95 percent are rats and mice. Dogs, cats, and primates, on which animal rights literature focuses, make up less than 2 percent of the one-half percent of animals used in science.

Animal rights fund-raising makes people believe that animal models involve dreadful pain to animals. They use misleading pictures of animals with electrodes in their heads, amputations, and so forth to "prove" the horrors of animal research. They have the audacity to imply, or actually claim, that no anesthetics or analgesics are used.

But according to a 1989 U.S. Department of Agriculture report[9], 93 percent of the animals used in research do not experience pain, or they have it relieved—either because the experiments do not involve pain (58 percent) or because the animals receive anesthesia or pain killers (35 percent). In the remaining 7 percent of the cases, anesthesia or pain killers cannot be given because they would interfere with the research results, such as studies to control chronic pain, a malady that afflicts some 30 million Americans.[10]

To mask their goal of the "total abolition of the use of animals in science," animal rightists focus on lurid (and fraudulent) claims of "abuse," often using photographs that turn out to be foreign, decades old, or staged. And they blur the distinction between biomedical research and consumer product safety testing in order to condemn the former with the testing procedures of the latter. But a hard look at consumer safety testing shows that it is a legitimate example of animal use in science.

A favorite target of animal rights fund-raising is the Draize eye irritancy test. It has everything: it uses rabbits (a lot more cuddly than rats) and it involves the eyes (extremely sensitive).

The test enables us to identify—humanely—many hazards to our eyes that cannot be caught by *in vitro* ("test tube") tests. In the test, a minute sample of the test material is applied to one eye of a rabbit, which is then compared with the other.

To exploit the public's ignorance of research protocols, animal rights groups have come up with a number of lies about the Draize test:

LIE: The Draize test is done without anesthetic.

TRUTH: The very first step in the Draize test is administration of an ocular anesthetic, except in very rare cases when it would change the results of the test.

LIE: The Draize test melts rabbits' eyeballs to test drain cleaner or bleach.

TRUTH: Caustic substances are screened out long before live animal tests. The first step is a review of prior experience through computer data banks such as the Cosmetic Ingredient Review. Anything known to be hazardous is eliminated at this level. Next come *in vitro* tests, starting with a litmus test. Substances with pH lower than 2.0 or higher than 11.5 are automatically labelled as hazardous to the eyes. That screens out corrosive substances. Next come newer *in vitro* tests, such as Eytex, a protein culture test. Anything with a Food and Drug Irritancy Index (FDII) greater than 5.0 is screened out. But substances that appear harmless (FDII of 5.0 or less) must be screened through the Draize test before widespread use.[11]

LIE: Rabbit eyes are too different from human eyes to yield useful results.

TRUTH: Rabbits are ideal subjects because the physiology of their eyes is similar to that of humans in every relevant way.

LIE: The test material is left in the rabbit's eye for days.

TRUTH: The eye is always rinsed out within fifteen minutes, and sooner if redness or swelling develops. The long "tear" lines shown running down from the rabbits' eyes in animal rights propaganda are not from tears, as they claim, but from this eyewash.

LIE: The Draize test is vain or frivolous, because it is used only to test cosmetics.

TRUTH: Children do accidentally get cosmetics into their eyes. Should they be the guinea pigs? In any event, the Draize test is used not just to test cosmetics, but also pharmaceuticals and other consumer products, including soap, eyedrops, contact lens solutions, skin-penetrating and burn-healing agents, anti-acne medications, sunblocks, and even some toys.

When animal rights groups tried to ban the Draize test in New Jersey, they were opposed by virtually every consumer and health advocacy group. Robert F. Corso, managing director of the American Lung Association of New Jersey, testified, "This [Draize] test is necessary for developing data required for the protection of consumers and workers by a variety of federal agencies including the Food and Drug Administration."[12]

Murray E. Bevan, chairman of the Government Affairs Committee of the New Jersey Affiliate of the American Diabetes Association, said, "We believe the elimination of the Draize test limits the many benefits which flow to diabetics and the general public from this important research tool. In fact, many of the research advances in the management and treatment of diabetes through the use of insulin could not have occurred without animal research methods like the Draize test."[13]

Animal rightists also tried to outlaw the Draize test in California. The California legislature adopted legislation to ban the use of ocular tests, including the Draize test, and skin irritancy tests on live animals for testing cosmetics and household products in 1991, but it was vetoed by Governor Pete Wilson. A similar bill had been vetoed by Governor George Deukmejian, Wilson's predecessor, the year before. In 1990, Senate Bills 30 and 40 were introduced into the Maryland General Assembly, which were similar to the California bills. The Maryland bills were also defeated.

Although the New Jersey, California, and Maryland bills failed, they required scientific and other groups to spend scarce resources and time to defeat the measures. Again, animal rightists take a toll on medical research. Even when they lose, they advance.

Animal rights groups often claim that the FDA does not require Draize testing of new products. The FDA is always looking for ways to reduce the number of animals used in testing. But despite intensive research, some hazards still escape even the best *in vitro* tests. "With respect to the Draize test, it is the FDA position that the Draize eye irritancy test is currently the most meaningful and reliable method for evaluating the hazard or safety of a substance introduced into or around the eye," according to Dr. Gerald B. Guest, director of the FDA's Center for Veterinary Medicine.[14] He adds, "Work toward alternatives is encouraged by the FDA," but warns, "There are presently no non-animal tests available to replace the Draize."

Animal rights groups spread similar misconceptions about all consumer safety testing. A case study is provided by PeTA's campaign against General Motors (GM), which uses animals in safety research and has in the past used them in head injury studies.

Every year between 400,000 and 500,000 Americans with head injuries are admitted to hospitals. Every five minutes one of these people dies. The injuries cause permanent and often devastating disability, such as blindness, deafness, loss of memory, emotional instability, learning problems, and epilepsy.[15]

Using animals in brain injury research has given scientists precious new knowledge. In the past, physicians believed that there was little that could be done medically at the time of an injury. Thanks to research on animals, they now know that if a brain-injured patient is treated immediately through aggressive medical procedures in addition to surgery, recovery is likely.

Animal experimentation in automobile tests has also led to such life-saving developments as child-restraint systems, air bags, the three-point shoulder harness, the energy-absorbing steering column, and the self-aligning steering wheel. And it has helped alleviate the effects of fumes from diesel and alternative fuels on the respiratory system and test the potential toxicity of new materials proposed for use in automobiles or automotive manufacturing processes.

Ingrid Newkirk claims that computer models and dummies are sufficient for automobile tests. But such tests are not adequate. GM has been singled out by PeTA, which has picketed its showrooms and meetings. If animal rightists succeed in forcing GM to cease experiments on animals for safety's sake, they will have sounded a death knell for many accident victims.

Ironically, PeTA criticizes GM for relying on animals rather than dummies. But GM does use dummies in crash tests—because, originally, GM used animals to develop the test dummies that are now employed by the entire automobile industry.

PeTA propaganda to the contrary, GM no longer uses animals in crash tests, but to test the toxicity of alternative fuels and automobile construction materials.

Yet the animal rightists have crippled such tests. In 1992, California passed a law making it illegal to use the results of animal testing in any liability suit involving automobiles. This will hamstring the development of cleaner fuels and lighter, safer cars, and will increase the cost of automobile insurance in California, and of cars nationwide. The greatest cost will be the loss of life.

An equally dangerous attack by animal rightists has been launched on toxicity testing. They focus on the classical Lethal Dose 50 (LD-50) test, which determines the maximum safe dose of a substance. In the original test, the dosage of a test substance was gradually increased in the diets of 40–100 rats or mice until half of them died.

Today, the classical LD-50 has been largely replaced with a "range limit" test, in which only 4–10 rats or mice are used. But a modified LD-50 still is absolutely necessary for new pharmaceuticals to determine at what dose the potential risks of a new treatment for cancer, or AIDS, or whatever, outweigh the benefits, and for finding appropriate emergency treatment in case of accidental poisoning or overdose.

"Although there are promising advances being made in the development and validation of nonanimal toxicology tests, these tests are not yet available on any widespread basis as replacements for whole laboratory animal models," according to Dr. Thomas Hamm, of the Division of Laboratory Animal Medicine at Stanford University School of Medicine. "There are severe limitations with nonanimal methods."[16]

As former U.S. Surgeon General C. Everett Koop put it, "There is no substitute for animal testing if we are to ensure the safety of all consumer products, from personal care and household cleaning products to health care and prescription drugs."[17]

Even Alan M. Goldberg, director of the Johns Hopkins Center for Alternatives to Animal Testing (CAAT), agrees: "I cannot recommend that the industry cease animal testing immediately. Until nonanimal tests are proven to be at least as effective as animal tests—and they have not yet—companies must continue to use animal tests to fulfill their moral and legal obligations to insure the safety of their products."[18]

"In safety testing as well as in basic biomedical research," says Dr. Goldberg, "it should be recognized that *in vitro* methods act in concert with whole animal studies to advance science, develop new products and drugs, and to treat, cure and prevent disease."[19]

If your child ingests something dangerous, you depend on your local poison control center to save your child's life. But how do the people at the poison control center know what to do?

The American Association of Poison Control Centers supports the safety testing of consumer products to determine the toxicity of these products prior to their introduction to the marketplace. This information is important for poison control centers to use to evaluate emergency medical situations involving inappropriate exposures in humans.

—American Association of Poison
Control Centers

Hundreds of times each day, the staff of the poison control center are called upon to assess the potential risk to the health of children and adults who are exposed to consumer products either by ingestion, inhalation, or skin contact. . . . The information that we must rely upon is derived from animal studies.

—Dr. Anthony S. Manoguerra,
Regional Poison Control Center
University of California, San Diego

I have personally treated or evaluated the reports of literally hundreds of thousands of children who have ingested household chemicals and cosmetics. The fact that few children die of these exposures is a result of research—including animal research—conducted over the years in industrial, government, academic, and clinical settings.

—Dr. Toby L. Litovitz, Director
National Capital Poison Control
Center

The Consumer Federation of America opposes efforts to outlaw the use of animals for the purposes of testing the safety of consumer products, such as household substances, drugs and cosmetics. Outlawing animal testing . . . would make it impossible to determine the adverse effects of many chemical ingredients used in thousands of consumer products.

—Consumer Federation of America

Perhaps the most harmful false claim in animal rights literature is that animal testing doesn't work. In support, the activists tout the Thalidomide tragedy. Thalidomide was prescribed during the 1960s in Europe for pregnant women suffering from morning sickness. But scientists soon learned to their horror that the "wonder drug" caused terrible birth defects. By the time the drug was banned, about ten thousand babies had been born with birth defects.

Animal rightists claim that Thalidomide was animal tested and approved by the FDA. But the FDA never approved Thalidomide for marketing in the United States because it believed the safety data collected by European manufacturers were inadequate. Further animal studies demonstrated that Thalidomide was a teratogen, or cause of birth defects. If more extensive animal studies had been conducted earlier, European governments would not have approved Thalidomide and thousands of babies would not have been born deformed.

Although birth defects from Thalidomide did not show up in rats, they did appear in rabbits and hamsters; final confirmation resulted from testing on rhesus monkeys. This tragedy was caused not by too much, but too little animal testing.

Animal rights activists claim that we cannot apply animal study results to humans. Animals do differ in their physiology, and occasionally one species may have an aberrant reaction to a drug. But valid extrapolation based on studies of at least two different species dramatically reduces this danger.

Today, if a substance appears harmless from animal tests, it goes on to clinical trials with human volunteers. Only 5 percent of products tested at the *in vitro* level are allowed to proceed to animal tests. Even so, 98 percent of these are stopped at the animal level, so they never proceed to humans. If we abolish this level, we would have to skip directly from *in vitro* to human trials. Outlawing animal tests would mean many more Thalidomide tragedies.

Animal testing is essential not only for consumer safety, but for environmental protection. According to Dr. Benjamin Trump, chairman of the Department of Pathology at the University of Maryland, the Chesapeake Bay has become cleaner in recent years primarily because new consumer products (such as nonphosphate detergents) have been developed that do not disrupt marine life. Prohibition of the animal tests that made such developments possible would hinder further attempts to clean our environment.[20]

Yet many corporations are lobbying to relax consumer protection laws so they can use cheaper (but less reliable) nonanimal tests. Some of these companies advertise that they are "cruelty free" because they do no animal testing when, in fact, they sell products that have been animal tested by others.

The Body Shop, for example, attracts millions in sales with its slogan, "AGAINST ANIMAL TESTING." But the fine print waffles: "No ingredient is used by The Body Shop that has been tested on animals within the last 5 years." In other words, The Body Shop, which is fifteen years old, is now selling products that were tested on animals during two-thirds of the company's self-righteous against-animal-testing campaign.

Many so-called "cruelty free" companies support animal rights groups that attack their competitors and lobby against consumer safety in general. The Body Shop publishes pamphlets advertising PeTA[21] and telling schoolchildren, "You can change things. . . . Why not mention the subject in school to your teacher. . . ?"[22]

To be fair, the suggestion by animal rights groups that bureaucratic rigidity causes excessive animal testing is plausible. After all, FDA approval absolves a manufacturer of most liability. Strict liability tort reform, insurance sanctions, and the discipline of the market would force companies to use the most accurate, rather than just the most governmentally approved, test methods. But the most accurate tests generally involve animals.

Animal rights groups, of course, want to ban all animal research as well as testing.

Today's animal rights groups aren't the first to claim animal models don't work. In 1875, Britain's Sir George Duckett of the Society for the Abolition of Vivisection declared, "Vivisection is monstrous. Medical science has little to learn, and nothing can be gained by repetition of experiments on living animals."[23] Today, PeTA repeats: "Contrary to what most people think, the bulk of animal experimentation consists of duplication, painful, costly and unnecessary forms of research."[24]

To be sure, given the vast amount of medical research, some duplication will inevitably occur. But sometimes duplication is necessary. The scientific method requires that for a conclusion to be accepted as scientific fact, test results must be duplicated by different experimenters. What works for one scientist may not work for another—the first researcher may not have detected some error.

As a practical matter, such duplication is limited because research money is scarce. And the "peer review" process avoids funding projects that duplicate other research for no good reason or because they seem to lack scientific promise. For example, the National

Institutes of Health (NIH), the largest source of support for bio-medical research in the United States, is able to fund only about one-fourth of all research proposals that it believes worthy of scientific investigation. NIH is not going to duplicate old projects when so much new science is waiting on the sidelines.

Just think of all the medical advances since Sir George intoned his pronouncement: vaccines for polio, smallpox, rubella, diphtheria, whooping cough, tetanus, tuberculosis, cholera, mumps, chickenpox, measles, and yellow fever; treatments for cancer, Hodgkin's disease, river blindness, jaundice, beriberi, pellagra, leprosy, hypertension, ulcers, asthma, arthritis, epilepsy, and mental illness; plus such miracles as anesthesia, chemotherapy, tranquilizers, antibiotics, transplantation, and monoclonal antibodies. (See appendix 4.) Millions of lives have been saved over the past century because Mr. Duckett failed to stop medical research. How many innocent people will suffer and die over the next century if today's animal rights movement succeeds?

The greatest threat to patients dependent on research today is the Physicians Committee for Responsible Medicine (PCRM), an animal rights group that masquerades as a health-advocacy group. It is actually funded by PeTA and headed by PeTA's scientific advisor, Neal Barnard.

Because health care workers willing to lend credence to animal rights are so few, those who do must pretend to an "expertise" in a wide range of areas. For example, after a break-in at a lab studying Sudden Infant Death Syndrome, PCRM provided an "expert" critique of the lab's work by Dr. Stephen Kaufman—an ophthalmologist (an eye specialist). And at a hearing in Pennsylvania, a gynecologist (a specialist on female reproductive organs) testified, not surprisingly, that she had never relied on information from the Draize eye irritancy test to treat her patients![25]

The worst offender on this score is Barnard himself, who regularly pontificates against dissection and claims the consumption of meat, eggs, and dairy products is carcinogenic. He even says that animals are counterproductive to diabetes research. Dr. Barnard is not a teacher, researcher, nutritionist, cancer specialist, internist, or even a general practitioner: he is a psychiatrist.

PCRM's most destructive campaign so far has been the attack on Dr. Michael Carey of the Louisiana State University (LSU) Medical School in New Orleans.

Dr. Carey's research involved finding better ways to care for people with head wounds. More than fifteen thousand people die from gunshot wounds to the head each year in the United States, yet knowledge of how to treat these injuries has advanced very little since World War II.[26]

The army recognized the importance of Carey's work and awarded him a $300,000 contract to investigate brain wounds in cats. In 1985, an additional $1.8 million contract was awarded, for a total of $2.1 million.

PCRM attacked the study, claiming falsely that the cats were not anesthetized. In response, Louisiana Congressman Bob Livingston requested an investigation of the army contract by the General Accounting Office (GAO), the investigative arm of Congress.

A seven-member committee of neurosurgeons reviewed the study and concluded that the project should continue because it "addressed critical scientific problems" and the approach was "well conceived, proper, and made maximum effort to protect the welfare of animals."[27] The army, LSU, and the American Association of Neurological Surgeons affirmed that the project was worthy and that Carey should continue with his work.

That was the wrong answer. In November 1989, Congress cut off funds for the research, pending the GAO report. In 1990, the GAO issued a report criticizing the findings of the research, based on the opinions of veterinarians with no experience in neurological research. In 1990, the army halted Dr. Carey's work in response to political pressure.

Thus PCRM was responsible for ending research that would have saved many lives. As American soldiers prepared for combat in Desert Storm, Dr. Michael Carey, a Purple Heart recipient and National Guard officer, was forced to abandon his research on brain wounds. Carey treated four ballistic head wounds and five blunt-trauma brain injuries during the hundred days that his unit served in that conflict. "Here we were in 1991, sending 'star wars' missiles to intercept SCUD [missile] launches from Iraq, with computers fighting many of the battles, and we still didn't know how best to treat even bullet wounds to the extremities," he lamented.[28]

Thanks to PCRM's campaign, American soldiers who might have been saved died.

Although PCRM claims to speak for physicians, the total membership of this group is a fraction of 1 percent of the physician population of the United States, and by PCRM's own admission, physicians constitute less than 10 percent of the total group membership. Because Barnard will not release PCRM's membership, we cannot verify that *any* member other than Barnard is a physician.[29]

PCRM's positions are definitely fringe. In a 1988 AMA survey, 99 percent of physicians agreed that animal experimentation had contributed to medical progress, and 97 percent supported the use of animals for basic research. In 1990, the AMA House of Delegates passed Resolution 109, which states:

> RESOLVED: That the American Medical Association register strong objections to the Physicians Committee for Responsible Medicine for implying that physicians who support the use of animals in biomedical research are irresponsible, for misrepresenting the critical role animals play in research and teaching, and for obscuring the overwhelming support for such research which exists among practicing physicians in the United States.[30]

Physicians are frightened by the deadly consequences to public health of widespread acceptance of animal rights myths. They are labeling PCRM the way the Surgeon General describes cigarettes: "Warning: This product is dangerous to your health."

Physicians have been using animals in medical treatment and research for more than two thousand years. In the third century B.C., philosopher and scientist Erisistratus reported using animals to study body functions. Five centuries later, Roman physician Galen examined apes and pigs to prove that veins carry blood rather than air.

In our days, scientists have come to rely on animal experimentation for cures to many diseases that imperil human beings. One of the first modern successes was the experimental work of Louis Pasteur, who searched for a vaccine against rabies. For his experiments, he used dogs infected with rabies—sure death to animal or human. Pasteur discovered that by using a weakened strain of the virus, he could save people who had been bitten by rabid dogs.

From Pasteur's day to the present, animal research has had a long and distinguished record of success. *Virtually every medical advance of the last century has hinged on studies involving animals.*[31] They have increased our life expectancy by some twenty-eight years.

Today, animal experiments are essential to research on AIDS, a disease that threatens to kill millions of people. "We'd be in absolute, utter darkness about AIDS if we hadn't done decades of basic research in animal retroviruses," says former U.S. Surgeon General C. Everett Koop.[32] The same is true of cancer, heart diseases, and strokes, which cause many more deaths than AIDS.

The most shameful tactic of animal rights is the insidious exploitation of innocent children. In 1985, the Animal Rights Coalition Conference (ARCC) published an internal document entitled "Action for the Animals: A Rising Tide." This how-to plan urged that activists "Get people into elementary and high schools to convince students about the evils of vivisection—gain entrance by developing 'how to take care of your pet' programs and then use entry to acquaint students with animal-rights issues."[33]

PeTA, the Animal Legal Defense Fund, and even the ASPCA are among the groups urging children to refuse to participate in classroom dissection. Dissection, of course, is the only way to really study anatomy. As biology teachers can attest, when students actually experience dissection, they suddenly regard biology as much more vital, as a "real" and profound experience.[34]

Students need not only theoretical learning but manipulative skills as well. Biology professor Thomas R. Lord at Indiana University of Pennsylvania observes: "They [students] handle the structure, feel its weight, probe its consistency, and explore its composition."[35] He knows from experience that such a study is not possible for a student behind a computer.

American students are consistently testing poorly in science achievement against their peers in other industrialized countries. The federal government projects a shortfall of 700,000 scientists in the United States by the year 2000.[36] Not enough students are being turned on by science education. Between 10th and 12th grades, the number of students taking sciences drops 50 percent.

The National Science Foundation reported that the hands-on activities in science classes have dropped between 15 and 27 percent (depending on the grade level). One of the major reasons for the drop is the decline in biology class dissection, for which animal rightists have been partially responsible.[37]

Barbara Bentley, a biology teacher at the State University of New York at Stony Brook, observed: "What seriously concerns me is we are going to find out that dissection is going to go the way of evolution."[38]

The animal rights approach to children is extremely deceptive. "Never appear to be opposed to animal research," John McArdle, formerly of HSUS, now with NEAVS, advises activists; "claim that your concern is only about the source of the animals used."[39] Activists maintain that the dogs and cats used in medical and veterinary training are stolen pets. They then prevent animal shelters from providing unclaimed animals (destined to be killed) to the schools—a tactic they call "pound seizure."

"After a successful pound seizure campaign, groups can then work to pass other laws eliminating various kinds of animal research," advises the ARCC: "A successful pound campaign can serve as an opening wedge for introducing other laws to eliminate animal research."[40]

Animal activists' first win was in Massachusetts, which banned use of pound animals in research. In 1987, New York State followed with a law prohibiting the release of any dog or cat from any type of shelter except for adoption or return to its owner. In 1991, Wright State University School of Medicine had to fight off efforts by the local humane society to ban the provision of unwanted pound animals to the university.

The public disagrees with this policy. Animal rightists sought to ban the provision of pound animals to the University of California at San Diego in 1990, when a proposition was put on the ballot, but it was overwhelmingly defeated by 68 percent of the vote.

For each dog or cat used in research, about fifty are killed in shelters. Eliminating the productive use of unclaimed animals places additional burdens on these shelters; moreover, schools must obtain purpose-bred animals for education, meaning twice as many animals die. But most disastrously, it increases the cost of research and training.

The patients' organization, incurably ill For Animal Research (iiFAR), in a study with the Illinois Society for Medical Research, determined that nationwide about 104,300 dogs and 50,000 cats are obtained annually from pounds for use in research. If the animals had to be purchased from breeders, the cost of research would increase by at least $80 million each year. "To put that number into perspective," the study reveals, "the American Heart Association awarded $56 million in research grants during 1986."[41]

This is a serious threat. Robert J. White, professor of neurosurgery at Case Western Reserve University, says that working on animals is the only way for medical students to learn how to handle surgical instruments and control bleeding. Cadavers can be used in some classes, but, as he points out, "cadavers don't bleed, and they don't wake up."[42]

Most adults would rather have doctors practice on animals before using these techniques on them. That's why, according to an Associated Press survey, 81 percent of Americans support the use of animals in medical training.[43]

As for doctors, in 1989, the AMA conducted a survey of more than 1,500 physicians to determine their attitudes about animal use in medical research and teaching. Nearly 90 percent reported that they had used animals during their formal medical education. Among all physicians, 91 percent thought that the use of animals had been important for their own training, and 93 percent supported the continued use of animals in medical education.[44]

The Human/Animal Liberation Front (HALF) advises activists combating research to "concentrate on cats, dogs and primates so as to ensure public sympathy."[45] But scientists use only three or four dogs and one cat per 100,000 research animals, and primates make up less than half of 1 percent of all the animals scientists use. Ninety to 95 percent are rats and mice, which, of course, the activists don't want you to know.[46]

Yet these few dogs, cats, and primates have been enormously important in understanding health problems. For example, cancer—especially mammary cancer—is prevalent in cats. Cats have helped develop and test new forms of therapy for breast cancer which afflicts one woman in eleven.

Similarly, the most common fatal disease for domestic cats today is leukemia. Researchers are using knowledge from cats to develop early warning tests for human leukemia. Similarly, feline AIDS provides researchers with one of the few models for aspects of AIDS in people.

Researchers have studied dogs for rabies and rickets. They have studied chickens for beriberi and the therapeutic use of streptomycin; monkeys for cancer chemotherapy, prevention of rubella, and corneal transplants; rabbits for poliomyelitis and sulfa drugs; and rodents for DNA and aureomycin.

Cats are among the most useful animal models for neurological research. But researchers like Sharon L. Juliano, a medical researcher and associate professor of anatomy at the Uniformed Services University of the Health Sciences in Bethesda, Maryland, are targeted by animal rights extremists for doing this work. Juliano's research developed from her work as an occupational therapist. She wanted to help people who had lost movement as a result of a stroke or traumatic injury. She herself had suffered such an injury in 1981 when her back was broken in a car accident. As a result, she is partially paralyzed in both legs and walks with a cane. If her work is successful, it could lead to a treatment for Alzheimer's, according to Robert H. Wurtz, president of the Society for Neuroscience.[47]

In 1991, animal rights extremists falsely accused her of mistreating animals. Since then, once a week a small group of demonstrators holds vigils outside her home in Kensington, Maryland. The protesters carry posters showing a wide-eyed kitten and animal parts dripping blood. They hand out leaflets in her neighborhood depicting her as cruel.

Juliano's magazine subscriptions were canceled by someone speaking in her name without her consent, and she received dozens of others she never ordered. A funeral home called saying that someone had given her name to make arrangements for a dead relative who, chillingly, was not dead.

The protesters say that they will not stop until Juliano quits her experiments on cats. The extremists never give up. But neither does Dr. Juliano.

Animal rights extremists deny that the gains of animal research have done anything to improve conditions for cancer, heart disease, or any other disease. But people with cancer live longer now than before animal research on the disease. Heart attacks used to be fatal at age fifty. But now, thanks to new surgical procedures to open clogged arteries and bypass surgery—both developed through animal research—millions of lives have been saved.

Animal rights terrorists are often oblivious to the damage they cause. In August 1987, for example, a group called the Band of Mercy broke into a research facility of the U.S. Department of Agriculture at Beltsville, Maryland, and stole seven African mini pigs and twenty-seven cats. The cats were infected with toxoplasmosis, a bacteria harmless to the cats, but potentially harmful to people, and the Centers for Disease Control had to issue a public health alert for the Washington, D.C., area.

Animal rightists are strangely silent on the use of animal models in veterinary medicine. As Charles Darwin commented about Pasteur's work on rabies, animal research to help people often helps animals even more.[48]

Animals treated for hookworm, heartworm, Giardia, tuberculosis, rickets, white muscle disease, brain tumors, birth defects, and cancer all benefit from animal research. It saves dogs from distemper, parvovirus, infectious hepatitis, parainfluenza, and leptospirosis; and cats from rhinotracheitis, pneumonitis, feline leukemia, enteritis, and dilated cardiomyopathy. It provides treatment for poultry with Newcastle disease, Marek's disease, fowl cholera, duck hepatitis, hemorrhagic enteritis, fowl typhoid, and fowl pox; horses with strangles, tetanus, and encephalomyelitis; sheep with anthrax and bluetongue; and pigs with influenza and swine erysipelas.

The ALF activists who firebombed the veterinary diagnostic clinic at the University of California at Davis couldn't care less about the animals it might have saved, any more than they cared about the $5 million the raid cost taxpayers.

Animal rights groups also claim that no laws regulate research. This is simply not true. In the United States, for example, federal law requires that a veterinarian be consulted when planning an experiment and that anesthetics, tranquilizers, and analgesics be used except in those instances when their use would interfere with the results of the experiment.

Federal regulations for the care of dogs and cats were adopted after the Laboratory Animal Welfare Act of 1966. Amendments to that law (now known as the Animal Welfare Act) have broadened and expanded it to include many other animals.

Federal law and regulations over the past few decades provide protections against animal abuse by all researchers who receive funding from the NIH and other federal agencies. They include cage sizes, feeding and watering, lighting, and sanitation for animals kept in laboratories. An animal care oversight committee—which must include at least one veterinarian, one nonscientist, and one person not affiliated with the institution conducting the research—supervises the conditions of the animal research. It has the legal authority to suspend any research project involving animals if it so deems, and to report it to the U.S. Department of Agriculture and to any federal agency funding the project, such as the NIH.

State and local governments have also adopted their own laws and regulations dealing with the humane treatment of animals. In addition, the professional medical societies have written their internal guidelines for the use of animals in research.

Regrettably, there will be cases of carelessness or laziness in medical research, as anywhere else, but neglect is the extreme exception and not the rule. Because a few schoolteachers abuse children does not mean we should ban schools. And because a few incompetent scientists mistreat animals does not mean that we should abandon essential medical research to find cures for human beings—and animals, too.

But animal rights groups are determined to ban animals in science. In both consumer product safety testing and biomedical research, they claim that nonanimal models are more effective than whole animal models. They propose existing adjuncts to animal research as "alternatives" to it: *in vitro* research, clinical research, epidemiologic studies, and computer modeling. Yet none of these so-called alternatives could possibly replace the need for animals. In fact, in many cases they even *increase* the need.[49]

"*In vitro*" literally means "in glass" but scientists interpret the term to include all sorts of research that does not involve live animals. *In vitro* testing involves a variety of living systems—bacteria, cultured animal and human cells, fertilized chicken eggs, or frog embryos—that are employed, generally in glass petri dishes or test tubes, to evaluate the toxicity of chemicals in human beings.

No financially responsible company would do any animal testing if it could possibly avoid it. According to *Toxicology: The Basic Science of Poisons*, the typical cost of a two-year chronic toxicity test in rats is $600,000. Any corporation out to make a profit has a built-in incentive to use the far cheaper *in vitro* tests whenever possible. Manufacturers have spent millions developing such techniques.

Not only have animal rights groups spent virtually nothing on such work, they have actually hindered it. Dr. Karen Chou of Michigan State University in East Lansing, for example, lost a decade of work on her *in vitro* models in 1992 when an ALF arson destroyed computer disks containing her workbook records.[50]

The most important *in vitro* adjunct so far is the Ames test, which identifies potential mutagens and has largely been responsible for a 40 percent decline in the annual number of lab animals used since 1968. But the test's inventor, Dr. Bruce Ames, a scientist at the

University of California at Berkeley, warns that "it's not a replacement" for whole animal testing. There is still a virtually endless list of known toxins, carcinogens, and teratogens that are not yet detectable by nonanimal methods.[51]

Cell cultures can indicate positive or negative chemical reactions and provide clues about what direction research should take. But the human body is complex. Drugs are distributed through the body by the circulatory system and can change in the process. Drugs affect many organs, such as the kidney, liver, stomach, intestines, heart, and lungs. Consequently, a drug may produce complex effects in a human being that are highly different from the simple effects it produces in a cell culture.

If you tried to make a simple cell culture as intricate as an animal—to test these complex reactions—you'd end up testing on an animal! You can't win at that game, and there's no way that cell cultures can become a total substitute for animal experiments.

Activists also recommend "clinical research," which is knowledge gained from studying people who are ill with particular diseases. This type of research (using new scanning technology) has isolated abnormalities in the brains of victims of Alzheimer's disease, epilepsy, and autism.

That's fine as far as it goes, but clinical research is severely limited as a scientific research tool. For example, generally the use of animals in medical experimentation is *superior* to the use of human beings. First of all, you can control your test subjects for genetic and environmental factors. Next, you can experiment on one variable over and over until you are sure of your result—not a practical option with humans. And you can trust animals more than people. We all know that people sometimes tell their doctors they are taking medications when in fact they are not. Fred W. Quimby, director of research animals at Cornell University, observes: "People typically follow veterinarians' prescriptions more closely than they do their own doctors."[52] Equally important, animals can be kept free of all diseases except those that researchers want to study. Sick people often have many different kinds of infections, making it difficult to isolate the one under study.

Animal rights literature also touts "epidemiologic studies," which are comparative analyses of diseases in different human populations. The studies try to answer questions like: why are some people susceptible to a particular disease, such as heart attacks or cancer? Such studies are useful but they cannot, for example, control the multiple variables affecting the health of populations, nor can they help develop new surgical techniques.

And of course animal rights activists endorse computer modeling of humans or animals for testing and research. But even long-established commercial programs often don't work, let alone experimental software complex enough to try to predict how the body will react.

Dr. Arthur Guyton, a world-renowned researcher in cardiovascular physiology, is noted for developing one of today's most comprehensive computer models of physiology. When he began publishing his mathematical analyses of the circulatory system, he received many letters from animal rightists congratulating him that his model had made the use of animals in medical research unnecessary.

Guyton protested that his computer model had actually *increased* the need for animal research, because of the requirement to test the predictions of the model. Models are "beautiful adjuncts for experiments on animals—not replacements," he said.[53]

Computer models can help scientists observe and analyze. But they cannot produce new information. In the words of R.E. Burke, computer models "permit scientists to examine their observations of the natural world so as to clarify the meaning of those observations and to guide further research." In his view, research data that are fed into computers must "come from the real world. In the case of a great deal of biomedical research, those data come from experimental animals." Computer models, he concludes, are not part of a replacement strategy.[54]

Animal rights groups further suggest that research and testing would be unnecessary if we devoted more resources to prevention. To them this means banning meat, eggs, and dairy products from human diets, an idea opposed by everyone from the American Heart Association to the American Medical Association and the American Dietetic Association.

True, too much saturated fat and cholesterol is dangerous—so is too much water. But using no animal products is as unwise as drinking no water. It means deficiencies in protein, vitamin B_{12}, and minerals. Moderation is the key to good health.

Prevention is important. But what on earth can "prevention" do for children born with heart defects or other congenital diseases?

Along with prevention, animal rightists claim that improved sanitation and diet—rather than medical research—are responsible for our phenomenally improved infant mortality rate and life expectancy in this century. Of course, they are important. But our knowledge of diet and hygiene as a means of disease prevention is derived from studies in which animals were used. *All* knowledge of nutrition is derived from animal studies.

When pushed to the wall, animal rightists demand that people be used as research subjects in place of animals. PeTA's Ingrid Newkirk suggests the use of cadavers. Those already are used where appropriate, but dead bodies do not respond the same way as live ones.

John McArdle of HSUS suggests the use of brain-dead people. "It may take people a while to get used to the idea," he admits, "but once they do, the savings in animal lives will be substantial."[55]

Singer Doris Day, founder of the Doris Day Animal League, goes further: "I think they should experiment on murderers. . . . What the hell are they going to do for society to pay us back? They should do that for us."[56]

The idea of using prisoners as guinea pigs is worthy of Josef Mengele, the infamous Nazi doctor who experimented on Jews. There is nothing humane or ethical about this.

But the pressure is on. Due to animal rights lobbyists, in 1985, without any committee hearings on the subject, Congress quietly adopted amendments to the Omnibus Farm Bill of 1985. These amendments imposed new requirements for handling research animals.

New USDA regulations on research required by the law totaled 132 pages of text. The Agriculture Department estimated that it will cost the affected institutions $876 million in one time capital costs and $207 million in annual operating costs to comply with the regulations. The Foundation for Biomedical Research puts its estimates at $2 billion for compliance. Since the medical research budget has not increased proportionately, the money needed to meet the new requirements will have to be diverted from medical research.

The cost of terrorism may be even greater. According to a survey of 126 medical schools released in July 1990 by the Association of American Medical Colleges, fifty-four reported being told that their institution was the target of animal rights activities.[57]

In the five years leading up to the report, seventy-six schools reported losing more than $4.5 million and 33,000 labor hours because of demonstrations, break-ins, vandalism, delays in construction, and other incidents. The schools also reported 3,800 incidents of faculty and staff harassment, ranging from bomb and death threats to graffiti, picketing of homes, and threatening letters and telephone calls.[58]

The survey revealed that the activities of animal activists cost America's medical schools alone approximately $10 million between 1986 and 1991. Medical schools are now spending over $15 million annually for security and related efforts to defend their work. Faculty and staff spend an estimated 100,000 hours annually to fight activist efforts, including bomb threats and attempts to mislead the public by spreading false information about research.

But the greatest cost is the loss of researchers who leave the field because of the threats. In Defense of Animals (IDA) was linked to a series of threats against at least forty university presidents. In 1985, HALF demonstrators hurled an axe into the front door of the home of a principal investigator of the New York State Psychiatric Institute. After a series of bomb scares and death threats spray-painted on buildings, Northwestern University had to provide one professor of neurobiology with bodyguards.

In 1990, Walter Salinger, head of the University of North Carolina psychology department, became a target of animal rights extremists. A letter addressed to him and a trustee of the AMA read in part, "Your brain and your wife's brain will be drilled and burned like you are doing to our lovely animals."[59]

Protesters carried signs with Salinger's picture on it. They referred to him as "Dr. Slaughter." "People called my neighbors and described me as a monster and warned them to keep their kids and pets out of my way. It was just terrifying," he said.[60]

In April 1991, Dr. Frederick A. King, director of the Yerkes Regional Primate Research Center at Emory University in Atlanta, was mailed a package that ticked. It contained a clock along with a note that read, "Clocks are not the only things that tick, you SOB."[61]

In 1988, Richard Van Sluyters, a researcher at the University of California at Berkeley, was singled out by Cleveland Amory of the Fund For Animals as the cruelest and most worthless researcher in the United States. Van Sluyters began to receive death threats not only against him but against his children. He was apparently the target of a bomb which detonated prematurely and killed the bomber. Federal authorities informed him that writings in that person's possession indicated Van Sluyters would be killed by a bomb.[62]

A Columbia University researcher received a telephone call with the simple message, "We know where you live." Later, someone threw a pool of red paint in front of his house. In January 1990, his home was burned down. The daughter of another researcher returned home from school with a note reading, "We know who your daughter is."[63]

In June 1990, ALF admitted responsibility for a bomb that exploded in England under the car of a veterinary surgeon, forcing her through the window of the vehicle. Five days later, a bomb fell from under the car of a Bristol University researcher. According to the former assistant secretary of the FBI for domestic intelligence and terrorism, the researcher was unharmed, but a thirteen-month-old boy in a passing stroller was critically injured in the explosion.[64]

The animal rightists' attack on animal research is a smokescreen. The bottom line is antiscience, a Luddite manifestation. (The Luddites, who took their name from Ned Lud, a retarded millworker who smashed automated looms, were early nineteenth-century

British antitechnological terrorists.) Ingrid Newkirk says that if animal research were to produce a cure for AIDS, "we'd be against it."[65] Chris DeRose, founder of Last Chance for Animals, admits, "If the death of one rat cured all diseases, it wouldn't make any difference to me."[66] Tom Regan argues that if scrapping animal-based research "means there are some things we cannot learn, then so be it. We have no basic right not to be harmed by those natural diseases we are heir to."[67]

This is pure "technophobia," the fear of technology, a Luddite reversion. As Ms. Newkirk put it in a speech at Loyola University in 1988:

> I find that as I get older I seem to become more of a Luddite. . . . And hearing animal experimenters describing me as a Luddite—which I used to think I was not. And now I think Ned Lud had the right idea and we should have stopped all the machinery way back when, and learned to live simple lives.[68]

Michael W. Fox of HSUS argues that we should "dethrone science and technology as the guiding forces in the mastery of nature." German animal rightist Rudolf Bahro writes, "When will we Greens at last say loud and clear that our science—reduced to its professed intention of 'relieving the toil of human existence'—is in both structure and function just as fundamentally a work of the devil as is our financial system?"[69] He continues:

> Animal experiments occupy a central place in the material and spiritual edifice of our whole civilization. We are speaking here of one of those foundation stones whose removal could cause the whole house to collapse.[70]

While evoking a fantasy of the lion lying down with the proverbial lamb, in reality an animal rights regime would plunge us into a new Dark Ages, with mankind once again helpless before scourges like the Black Death.

Sydney Singer of the Good Shepherd Foundation writes, "If natural healing is not possible given the energy of the environment, it may be right for that being to change form, as eddy currents do, into another energy form. Some people call this death."[71]

When animal rights activists claim that researchers steal pets, or blind rabbits with drain cleaner, or don't use anesthetics, or do meaningless research, they lie. Their goal is not to improve science, but to destroy it. If they succeed, many more people and animals will face the brutal reality masked by the fantasy of animal rights.

5

ANIMAL AGRICULTURE
Let 'em Eat Tofu

In 1991, PeTA took out a full-page newspaper advertisement which began:

> Milwaukee . . . July 1991 . . . They were drugged and dragged across the room . . . Their legs and feet were bound together . . . Their struggles and cries went unanswered . . . Then they were slaughtered and their heads sawn off . . . Their body parts were refrigerated to be eaten later . . . Their bones were discarded with the trash. It's still going on.[1]

PeTA's ad was intended to evoke the crimes of Jeffrey Dahmer, the confessed serial murderer, child molester, and cannibal, who was then big news. PeTA's criticism, of course, was aimed not at Dahmer but at people who eat meat. When we eat chicken, steak, or fish, the "logic" goes, we are behaving exactly like Jeffrey Dahmer. The ad then pleads: "Please remember that scenario is reality for over 16 million sensitive individuals who lose their lives every day in this country for nothing more than the fleeting taste of 'meat.' " To PeTA, cows, pigs, and chickens are the equivalent of humans.

The ad implies that parents who feed their children meat risk turning them into murderers, and warns: "Non-violence can begin at breakfast, with what you eat."

PeTA's ad was particularly insulting to the parents of Dahmer's victims. PeTA first tried to place the ad in newspapers in Milwaukee, where Dahmer's murders took place, but the papers refused it. Next it turned to Des Moines, a major center of hog production.

PeTA paid the *Des Moines Register* $11,200 to run the ad. The public was outraged. The paper reportedly lost over $33,000 from canceled subscriptions and advertising. The ad drew criticism even from *Vegetarian Times* magazine and Michael W. Fox of HSUS, who called PeTA a "cult."

The animal rights attack on farming is a shock to most people. America feeds much of the world. Farmers make up only 2 percent of our population, yet they not only feed our fellow citizens but have an abundance left over for export. And when any catastrophe—famine, earthquake, civil war—disrupts a foreign country's food supply, food becomes our nation's ambassador of good will.

The world, and we ourselves, always assume that the United States will have a plentiful supply of food. Today, we take our agriculture for granted to such an extent that we pay little attention to where food comes from or how it is produced. We are, after all, a largely urban people.

Few Americans realize that abundant food is a luxury not shared by most people in the world. For example, European countries that lived under communism for much of the twentieth century experienced recurrent shortages of basic food. One of the remaining few communist countries, Cuba, is now advising its subjects to eat wild grasses and weeds.

Much of America's agricultural might comes from animals, such as cows, pigs, lambs, chickens, and turkeys; as well as marine animals, such as tuna, salmon, flounder, cod, shrimp, and oyster. An overwhelming number of Americans eat these animal foods. A 1992 survey reveals that only 7 percent of the American people identify themselves as vegetarians, and 80 percent of these say they eat fish or poultry. Most of the rest eat eggs and dairy products, which do not grow on trees.

Today, we Americans must question the future of our food supply. Because, if the animal rightists succeed, we will no longer be able to produce or consume animal products. No more hamburgers at McDonald's, steaks at Ponderosa, fried chickens at KFC, or shrimp dinners at Red Lobster. Nor could we buy lamb, turkey, steak, or pork at the supermarket, or milk at the convenience store.

Rough on the poor people in Third World countries, who would have to suffer natural disasters, poverty, or war, without being able to count on American animal agriculture.

To understand what will happen to us and to people who depend on us if the animal rights movement succeeds in its grand design, we need to look at animal agriculture in the United States and consider why our farmers have been so successful.

The United States is favored with good climate and fertile soil. But much of our success is also a tribute to the research, technology, science, and hard work of men and women as well as to stable political conditions and a dynamic economic system.

Perhaps most important is the care that U.S. farmers give to their animals. Farmers understand that if they are going to survive in a highly competitive business, they must watch their animals carefully. If farmers mistreat their stock or allow them to fall victim to disease, attacks by animal predators, or hunger, both the animals and the farmers will suffer.[2]

Farmers also know that they are dependent upon the environment for their economic well-being. If grasslands are exhausted so cattle cannot graze, ranchers will go out of business. So too, if the water supply dries up or becomes polluted. Farmers do not want to commit economic suicide. So they take precautions to preserve grasslands and to assure a sufficient and healthy supply of water for their animals.

Farmers go to great trouble to learn and apply proper agricultural techniques for each species based on its unique nature. This leads to distinctive solutions for housing, food, and care. Some animals are housed in barns to protect them against bad weather, predators, and disease. By putting these animals indoors rather than allowing them to roam freely, a farmer can better assure that each animal will obtain a proper diet and be supervised carefully for health purposes. Other animal species may require much outdoor space because of their special feeding needs.

When you know the facts about agriculture, animal rights objections turn out to be either naive or just plain false. Let's look at some of their favorite targets.

Start with the most obvious target, veal. Veal calves are the male progeny of dairy cows. They can't give milk, and since a single bull can suffice for a large herd of cows, most male calves are useless unless they are kept for veal. Before the development of a market for veal, the surplus male calves were all killed at birth.

Veal calves are raised in separate stalls, which allow farmers to monitor their diet and health, and protect the calves from their more aggressive siblings. The floors of the stalls are slotted to allow for the removal of waste. WHoop De Doo

Animal rights activists charge that veal calves are imprisoned in crates through a system of "solitary confinement"—kept in darkness and unable even to see other veal calves. They claim the calves are unable to move because they are chained in a small space. Finally, they contend that the veal calves caught up in such a system produce food that is unhealthy for consumers.

This description of veal farming is simply not true. In the modern stall system, veal calves can move. They lie down and stand up. They can see and react to other calves, although they cannot hurt one another. Veal barns are well lit and maintained in a sanitary condition. Veal feed is especially prepared for veal calves to give proper nutrition and health.

Why would farmers abuse a veal calf or any other animal that they depend upon for their livelihood? If the calves are mistreated, poorly fed, or kept in unhealthy surroundings, the animals will become diseased, malnourished, and may even die. Unless farmers take care of their animals, they will lose their calves and their financial investment.

Animal rights does not stop with veal. According to Mitchell Davis, executive editor of *Art Culinaire* magazine, in 1992, PeTA tried to close down Commonwealth Enterprises, a producer of *foie gras* in the Hudson Valley in the state of New York.[3]

Foie gras is made from the liver of Moulard duck. PeTA argued that the production process was cruel—that the ducks were force-fed until they "exploded"—and it sent literature to restaurants around the country to get them to stop serving *foie gras* and picketed two restaurants in Manhattan.

After investigation, the district attorney of Sullivan County in New York State dropped all cruelty to animal charges for lack of evidence. But PeTA continues to raise funds off the hoax, claiming that the exoneration of yet another victim is evidence of corruption.

PeTA opposes not just *foie gras*, but all poultry production. Like veal, poultry requires special agricultural techniques. Chickens are raised for their eggs or meat. Animal rightists criticize in particular the "debeaking" process (removing the sharp tip of the beak), which they term "cruel." In fact, chickens are debeaked because chickens are cannibals. Without provocation, chickens will attack and eat their fellow chickens.[4]

In the real world of farming, even animal rightists can become educated. When Farm Animals Concerns Trust (FACT), an animal rights group, raised free-range hens for nest eggs that it sold at Midwestern food stores, it discovered that it had a problem. According to Robert Brown, the founder of FACT, "When we started in 1984, our hens were not debeaked, but there was just too much cannibalism."[5] Animal rights literature nevertheless continues to condemn debeaking as an example of the human abuse of animals.

Animal rightists also claim that antibiotics and other medications used on chickens are unhealthy. In fact, pesticides and antibiotics are used to make chickens grow and produce efficiently. They protect the chickens, the farmers, and the eventual consumers. Federal agencies and inspectors regard pesticides and antibiotics as safe. All antibiotics are removed weeks ahead of the slaughter date so that no residue will be passed on to the consumer.

Americans are consuming ever-increasing amounts of chicken, apparently with no harmful results. Besides, producers know that they are subject to Department of Agriculture inspection. If they produce sick chickens, not only will they be closed down by the government but they will no longer be able to sell their products to consumers.

Animal rightists claim that chickens are overcrowded in their cages. Actually, chickens are kept in cages so their diet and water supply can be assured and egg collection can be efficient. And studies have shown that chickens congregate in one place no matter how much space they have. Farmers know that if they abandoned the battery cage or chicken house system and allowed chickens to roam freely, the free-range chickens would eat any kind of garbage they found rather than the good, clean, nutritious food that farm-caged chickens receive. "Free-range" chickens (what we used to call barnyard chickens) are subject to a great deal of disease, fighting, and cannibalism. Caged chickens are better off all around. A LIE.

Animal rightists assert that chickens suffer from having to stand on the wire mesh cage floor. Awful as it looks to us soft-soled humans, wire mesh flooring does not hurt a bird's claws. Wire mesh is used so the chickens' waste can be removed easily, minimizing disease.

PeTA's alternative to caging poultry is to kill it. When PeTA acquired a group of roosters for its Aspin Hill "sanctuary," the group was surprised to learn that cocks don't have to be "trained" or "abused" to want to fight. Cockfighting is an inherited trait. PeTA's method of making peace was to stage a mass killing of the birds in 1991. Two years later, PeTA was still reportedly killing healthy roosters. FALSE.

Animal rights activists tout their emotional claims about chickens not because chicken farmers are cruel or because chickens are harmful to humans, but because they do not want any animals to be eaten by people. Activists ignore the facts in order to promote their agenda.

Looking for a person to harass as a symbol of animal agriculture, animal rights activists zeroed in on Frank Perdue, the seventy-one-year-old president of Perdue chickens. Animal Rights International spearheaded a movement to get Frank Perdue removed from the Board of Regents of the University of Maryland—a voluntary position he held because of a commitment to community service.

In a full-page newspaper advertisement in the *Washington Times*,[6] the animal rights organization attacked Perdue's business dealings and accused him of abusing animals and ruining the environment. Then in 1992, a PeTA activist threw a pie in Perdue's face while he was attending a trustees meeting for the university. (It wasn't a chicken pie.)

Another facet of the poultry industry is eggs. Compare the way eggs were produced one hundred years ago with today. A century ago, nearly every family raised chickens in its own backyard. After a chicken had laid a relatively small number of eggs, it was killed and eaten. Even as late as the 1940s, small backyard flocks of one hundred chickens or less made up the majority of the egg-producing industry. Barnyard chickens—continuously subjected to diseases, freezing, predators, poisoning, and infighting—had a precarious existence and a mortality rate as high as 40 percent. The average yearly egg production in 1920 was only 112 eggs per hen, and many eggs were contaminated by the microbes from poultry diseases.

As more people moved into cities and suburbs, demand for eggs exceeded the supply, and the modern egg industry was born. Its strategy was to enlarge the size of the laying flocks and improve the laying efficiency of the hens.

The egg industry has since pioneered many improvements in layer flocks, including ways to reduce disease, improve nutrition, protect the chickens from physical harm, and strengthen their genetic makeup. Human ingenuity, responding to the law of supply and demand, has helped people—and the chickens are healthier to boot.— BUT NOT HAPPY

Cattle farming is another target of animal rightists, although they suffered a recent setback when their slogan "Cattle Free By '93" proved to be premature.

Cattle are raised on farms and ranches primarily for beef or dairy products. Beef has long been a staple of the American diet. We also consume cattle products other than beef, such as liver, brains, tripe, sausage, milk, butter, cheese, yogurt, and ice cream. Cattle products are rich in protein and contain vitamins and minerals that are not found in many vegetables or fruits.

Animal rightists seek to end all use of animals by humans, so they want to put an end to the cattle industry. Typically, they have devised a number of distortions to discredit cattle products. In a broad sweep, animal rightists blame beef for nearly every problem under the sun. In his book, *Diet for A New America*, John Robbins, heir to the Baskin-Robbins ice cream empire, writes that cows are responsible for everything from deforestation of the Amazon to the

Somali famine and global warming.[7] He claims that the book was "channeled" to him by a giant talking cow and pig that came to him in his dreams.[8] His son, Ocean, is touring the nation's schools, spreading this anticow propaganda through his children's performing troupe, Youth for Environmental Sanity! (YES!).

Jeremy Rifkin made a particularly sharp attack on the beef industry in his much ballyhooed book, *Beyond Beef: The Rise and Fall of the Cattle Culture.*[9] An environmentalist who is best known for his opposition to genetic engineering, Rifkin was an architect of the Beyond Beef Coalition in 1992. The coalition's goal is to reduce beef consumption 50 percent by the year 2000 in sixteen countries.

The objections of animal rightists like Rifkin and the Beyond Beef Coalition are based on specious arguments concerning animal welfare, human health, and the environment. At best, the arguments are misleading; at worst, they are falsehoods.

Animal rights advocates claim that ranchers are cruel, condemning the practices of dehorning and branding. The truth is that these techniques have been fine-tuned to assure the least amount of pain to the animals.

Both dehorning and branding are necessary. Cattle are dehorned to avoid injury to other cattle or to the rancher. Branding is necessary to ensure identification and thus to help maintain health records for cattle. The branding of cattle has been correctly likened to the vaccination of children. In both, there is short-term discomfort for long-term gain.

Animal rights advocates depend on popular ignorance to make their case convincing. Urban America is unfamiliar with the processes of beef production and agriculture in general. Recently when I was giving a speech, someone in the audience yelled, "Who needs these [expletive deleted] farmers? We can just go to the grocery store!"

The animal rights attack on farming is sheer hypocrisy. According to the *Village Voice*, Cleveland Amory's group, the Fund For Animals (FFA) purchases animals at livestock auctions for its animal "sanctuary" at the Black Beauty ranch near Dallas, Texas. FFA uses the ranch and such "rescued" animals to raise a great deal of money, as mentioned in chapter 2. But Black Beauty ranch manager Billy Saxon was recently caught running a hog and cattle business on the side. According to the article, Saxon intermingled his business with that of the sanctuary. He also admitted breeding FFA boars ("rescued" from slaughter) with his sows and then selling the offspring for slaughter.[10]

FFA's Wayne Pacelle acknowledged that he had been aware of the cattle-raising business for some time but said he had kept Saxon on because of his fine work at the ranch. Saxon finally was fired, and walked away with a pocketful of the "profits of death." Amory claimed to be shocked that anyone could believe that just because Saxon raised livestock for slaughter, he did not care about the animals. Yet Amory is the first to label every other livestock producer an animal "exploiter."

Meanwhile, FFA raised a bundle for its "sanctuary."

In order not to limit their attack to what they call a "moral" argument, animal rightists also claim consumer self-interest by depicting cattle products as unhealthy for human consumption. They initiate antibeef and antimilk campaigns based on health concerns.

The truth is that assertions about the danger of beef to health lack scientific credibility. For example, the Beyond Beef Coalition charges that "aside from smoking, there is no greater personal health risk than eating meat."[11] Assessing this claim, Jeanne Goldberg, an assistant professor of nutrition at Tufts University, said that "to talk about smoking and beef in the same sentence is nonsense."[12] She found a clear scientific connection between cigarettes and health problems but not between beef and disease. She did note some dangers of consuming too much meat, like consuming too much of anything. But no bona fide health expert is recommending that people give up beef.

Those concerned with health need to understand that, unlike tobacco, livestock products contain components that are essential for good health, such as protein, calcium, iron, zinc, and vitamins A and B_{12}.[13] Lean meat is so healthy, in fact, that it is recommended by such scientifically respected organizations as the American Heart Association and the American Dietetic Association.

Not only do animal rightists attack meat as unhealthy, they condemn milk as well. The Physicians Committee for Responsible Medicine (PCRM), an animal rights group, charges that milk should not be recommended in government guidelines. But every scientific analysis of cow's milk advocates its use for those over one year of age (infants should be fed mother's milk). Dr. Robert Kleinman, chairman of the American Academy of Pediatrics, notes: "There is no single perfect food, but milk is a major source of a number of important nutrients."[14]

Animal rightists specifically condemn milk because of its relatively high cholesterol and fat content. High cholesterol contributes to heart disease, so the argument is superficially plausible. But when animal rightists condemn milk for its fat content, they fail to take into account that nutritionists and pediatricians now uniformly recommend low-fat milk for all children.

Reluctantly accepting that milk contains healthy components, animal rights advocates trot out "substitutes." PCRM endorses broccoli or kale as replacements, but Carole Sugarman, a food writer for the *Washington Post*, expressed the common sense knowledge of most mothers about their kids' eating habits when she discovered that it takes about 1 1/2 cups of cooked broccoli or three cups of kale to equal the calcium in one cup of milk.[15] Just how many children will eat ten cups' worth of kale and broccoli a day? she asked wryly.

Getting down to the real bottom line, Dr. Isadore Rosenfeld noted, "People living in countries with the highest milk consumption have the longest life spans." She concludes that "milk really is a nearly perfect food."[16]

In order to heighten fear about all animal products, animal rightists focus on the danger to human health from alleged antibiotic residues in animal products. But federal agencies inspecting agriculture and scientists who do independent investigations know that these chemicals do not pose hazards to human health. The real hazard comes from people who don't wash their hands before preparing food.

Nor is there any danger from growth hormones that are given to animals—another fear raised by animal rights advocates. In fact, hormones also are used in vegetable products that are sold regularly in the supermarket—a subject rarely discussed by vegetarian proponents.

To put the matter into better perspective, according to researchers at Texas A & M University, a 3 oz. serving of hormone-treated peas contains 200 times the hormone estrogen of a 3 oz. serving of hormone-treated beef; and a 3 oz. serving of cabbage contains 1,000 times the amount of estrogen found in such beef.[17] It seems as if vegetarians who are concerned about hormones in their food have more problems than omnivores.

Obviously, the alternative to eating meat—vegetarianism—provides no guarantees to good health. Vegetarians must be very careful with their diets. They need to take vitamin supplements because a completely vegetarian diet lacks nutrients found in meat products—specifically, Vitamin B_{12} supplements. These are often taken in the form of spirulina, made from anaerobic yeast, an animal! Vegetarians also must worry about consuming such nonanimal products as tropical oil, sugar, caffeine, and salt. Those, too, can be harmful to health in excess.

Concerned about the health of Americans, since 1956, the U.S. Department of Agriculture (USDA) has published a list of essential food groups needed for a balanced diet—a list that includes meat and dairy products. Animal rightists have tried hard to get meat and dairy products dropped from the government's list, but they have been unsuccessful so far.

Animal rightists also base their case against cattle farming on pseudo-humanitarian concerns. They say that grain used to feed cows could be better consumed by starving people in developing countries. Once again, they build their case on straw. First, 80 to 85 percent of the feed used in cattle production is suitable only for animals, not for humans. Converting this fodder into meat actually increases the amount of food available for human consumption.[18]

Second and most importantly, the plight of the poor people of the world has nothing to do with cattle agriculture in the United States.

India, for example, experienced famines and was heavily dependent upon food assistance in the years after World War II even though it did not raise cattle for food. Today, however, India is largely self-sufficient in agricultural production, but only because it has introduced modern scientific methods to improve yields. Without animal agriculture, much of the grain now produced for feed would not be grown. The Third World would still starve, and the United States would experience an agricultural depression.

The reasons why so many developing countries remain poor are intricate and deep, but they have nothing to do with the cattle industry.

Finally, animal rightists complain about the cattle industry's depredations of the environment. They say that cattle are destroying our grasslands, that the methane gas cattle emit contributes to the problem of global warming, that our great demand for beef speeds up the destruction of the rain forests, and that ranchers are using up and polluting water.

Regarding overgrazing, animal rightists are hypocritical. When deer, buffalo, or any other wild animal increase in numbers so as to devour all the vegetation and damage the land, animal rightists ignore the environmental abuse. But when cattle graze in a manner that benefits the grasslands, they protest.

Chapters 7 and 9 deal with the nutria that are destroying the wetlands in Louisiana and the deer that are defoliating Catoctin National Park in Maryland. But while all of this natural environmental damage is going on, animal rightists condemn the sensible solution of reducing the animal population. For animal rights proponents, the environment seems to be just a propaganda tool, available to "save" animals but not a means for human and animal survival! With friends like animal rightists, true conservationists need no enemies.

As is sometimes the case, there may be a scintilla of truth to what animal rightists say about cattle overgrazing. Years ago, cattle were permitted to overgraze and damage some land. This was the exception rather than the rule, and is certainly not the case today. Today, since ranchers do not want to destroy scarce grazing land, they rotate their cattle among different grazing areas.

The real damage to grazing land would occur if the Beyond Beef crowd gets its way, given that its prescriptions deny the facts of nature. In effect, although foraging is beneficial, these people ignore the benefit to grasslands of grazing livestock. As ecologist Alston Chase notes, "Just as deer and cattle need grass, so grass needs deer or cattle. By trampling, ungulates [hoofed foragers, like cows] accelerate decomposition of vegetation, thus recycling vital nutrients. Through defecation, they spread seeds and fertilizer."[19] Chase adds that ending grazing altogether leads to desertification—loss of grassland—which is the very result that the antibeefers claim they want to prevent.

Animal rightists also pretend to insights on global warming. In the past few years various environmentalists have contended that the atmosphere of the earth is warming up fast. Carbon dioxide and other gases are supposed to be contributing to this condition. Many worry that unless something is done to reduce the temperature, our earth will experience environmental catastrophe. They call for drastic measures to deal with the "crisis," such as massive fuel taxes and rationing.

But a forty-year Russian and American study of over 27,000 actual temperature readings, published in *Nature* in 1993, found no evidence of global warming.[20] And a recent survey discovered that 82 percent of atmospheric scientists don't believe in global warming.[21] (Incidentally, many of the same proponents of this scare story were upset about "global freezing" a decade or so ago.[22])

Animal rights advocates generally claim that the U.S. beef industry is a major contributor to our imminent demise because of the methane gas that cows emit through their flatulence. Yet these same people ignore the fact that wild ungulates have the same digestive processes as their domestic counterparts. Dr. Dixy Lee Ray, a scientist and former chairman of the Atomic Energy Commission, notes that American cows produce about 50 million tons of methane and hydrocarbons. But she calculates that the largest source of greenhouse gases may well be termites, whose digestive activities are responsible for about 50 *billion* tons of carbon dioxide and methane annually.[23] U.S. beef cattle production is thus responsible, at most, for one-tenth of 1 percent of atmospheric methane gas, hardly a consequential factor in what is billed as an emerging ecological catastrophe.

If the animal rightists really wanted to do something about methane gas, they would be out there killing termites. That won't happen, because they are against pest control. So much for their concern for the environment.

Equally specious is the animal rightists' charge that America's demand for beef is responsible for the destruction of the world's rain forests. Environmentalists decry the destruction of these forests for many reasons, including the alleged effect on the global climate and the loss of rare plants and animal species.

But American beef-eaters are not the problem. Most of the meat that we consume is raised in the United States. In any event, the portion of the Amazon region that is being deforested is not used to raise cattle, but for subsistence farming, slash and burn agriculture, and harvesting wood for cooking fuel.

Nor is it true the U.S. beef industry causes a loss of water resources. On the contrary, most water in the West comes from watering holes dug by ranchers. They have actually increased the amount of water available to sustain riparian areas and wildlife—especially waterfowl that need wetlands.

Having lost every rational argument against animal husbandry, the animal rightists turn to violence. The Animal Liberation Front (ALF), jointly with Earth First!, firebombed the Dixon Livestock Company, and attempted firebombings of the California Cattlemen's Association in Sacramento, the Luce-Carmel Meat Company in Monterey, and the Northwest Farm Food Cooperative in Edmonds, Washington.[24]

Poultry farms have also been a target. ALF committed burglary at the Davis Poultry and Egg Ranch, and a group called the Farm Freedom Fighters committed burglaries at Sydel's Egg Farm (Hartley, Delaware) and Wolfe Poultry Farms (Milan, Pennsylvania).[25]

After decades of sponsoring tours of local livestock operations,

Illinois' Peoria County Farm Bureau stopped the tours because participating farmers were harassed by threatening phone calls and letters, and because their farms were assaulted by vandals. Equipment was tampered with, cattle hutches were overturned, and hay barns were set on fire.

ALF's spokeswoman Margo Tannenbaum of San Bernadino, California, says that the group's goal is "the elimination of the livestock industry." She adds: "The reason why the Animal Liberation Front is conducting economic sabotage to the poultry and livestock industries is to encourage those involved to quit and follow other pursuits."[26] In her mouth, "encourage" becomes a euphemism for "threaten."

It is hard to believe that good-hearted people could support such activities. American animal agriculture is humane; livestock farmers and ranchers are concerned with animal welfare and conservation; our meat, eggs, and dairy products are safe. And our life expectancy is longer and our mortality rate lower than at any other time in our history.

But animal rights opposition to animal agriculture is not really based on concerns for animal welfare, conservation, or human health. The bottom line is Ingrid Newkirk's belief that "eating meat is barbaric." Their objective is to eliminate all animal use—even if it means starvation.

6

PETS
Farewell to Fido

What would happen to "seeing-eye" dogs for the blind under an animal rights regime?

"[T]here is a profound need to reevaluate the entire guide dog industry," according to *The Animals' Voice* magazine. Writer Cole McFarland calls the training and use of guide, or seeing-eye, dogs "a paternalistic industry which treats animals as tools," and concludes, "Whether service and guide dogs receive a fair exchange for their labors is, of course, debatable."[1]

Jenine McKeown, former president of the Columbus, Ohio, chapter of the American Council of the Blind, reported in 1991 that while training a future guide dog "a member of FORWARD Working Dog Support Group, made up of guide-dog handlers and friends, was harassed and physically threatened" by an "animal rights activist."[2]

This is not an isolated case or an isolated issue. In 1988, for example, the Disney Company agreed to house sixty-five capuchin monkeys at no charge and build a $200,000 breeding facility near Discovery Island, a zoological park at Disney World. It was to be used by Helping Hands: Simian Aides for the Disabled, a group affiliated with Boston University.

These animals, which are sometimes known as "organ grinder" monkeys, are trained to perform tasks for paraplegics—people who are unable to use their arms or legs. The monkeys are taught to fetch food from a refrigerator and serve it, turn light switches on and off, retrieve books and magazines, and perform many other tasks that most of us do without difficulty. After training the monkeys, Helping Hands gives them to paraplegics at no charge.

The paraplegics find that the animals are indispensable and cannot be replaced by robots—the solution proposed by animal rights advocates. Gary Sprinkle, a paraplegic, spoke for others when he said, "Robots won't play. They won't jump around the living room or wrestle with the dogs. A robot would be pretty dull."[3]

Helping Hands designs procedures and training devices that take into account the quality of life of the monkeys as well as the people they are helping. It removes the monkey's teeth so the monkeys cannot bite the paraplegic, but the monkeys continue to eat the same diet since monkey chow is softened in juice.

Because a home contains items that can be dangerous when used recklessly—such as an electrical appliance—Helping Hands employs a system that allows the paraplegic to warn the monkey off, an instrument that alerts the monkey through electric buzzes. If the monkey touches an off-limit item, such as a lamp or medicine cabinet, it hears a warning buzz. If the animal does not move away, it receives a small jolt in its tail, administered from a belt worn by the monkey.

The jolt is equivalent to the sensation one gets from static when walking on a carpet on a dry day. It is not painful, and it rarely needs to be used once the monkey is settled into a paraplegic's home. The monkeys take good care of the paraplegics, and in return, the paraplegics are devoted to their animal friends.

Animal rightists deplore that kind of friendship. Friends of Animals in Connecticut and Primarily Primates of Texas, animal rights organizations, lobbied Disney to end its association with the program. After much pressure, the Disney Company agreed and asked Helping Hands to move its breeding colony off Discovery Island. But after thoroughly investigating the charges, the Disney Company reversed itself and the Helping Hands program, which would otherwise have died, continued.

The sort of pressure exerted can be gleaned from Leslie Fain, a Washington lobbyist for Friends of Animals, who referred to Helping Hands as a "misguided and cruel program" that exposed both the monkeys and their disabled masters to harm. "They are basically trying to create a little slave race," Fain told a reporter for the *Orlando Sentinel*. "Primates are wild animals and can never be domesticated."[4] The people who depend on these helpful, friendly animals disagree.

That these groups would take seeing-eye dogs from the blind and animal helpers from paraplegics should come as no surprise to anyone familiar with the animal rights movement. Animal rightists condemn the use of police canine patrols to capture violent criminals and even denounce the use of dogs by customs officials to seek out carriers of cocaine and other illegal drugs—drugs that would destroy the minds and lives of many people.

In effect, the animal rightists have declared war on pets. In its "Statement on Companion Animals," PeTA says, "As John Bryant has written in his book *Fettered Kingdoms*, [pets] are like slaves, even if well-kept slaves."[5] In the book, Mr. Bryant concludes: "Let us allow the dog to disappear from our brick and concrete jungles— from our firesides, from the leather nooses and chains by which we enslave it."[6]

People who are not familiar with the animal rights movement are surprised to learn that it is opposed to having pets. They read animal rights literature that is filled with pleas to end animal suffering. And they see photographs of animal rights leaders looking adoringly at dogs and cats.

But PeTA founder Ingrid Newkirk puts it plainly: "Pet ownership is an absolutely abysmal situation brought about by human manipulation."[7] If she has her way, she told *Harper's* in August 1988, "eventually companion animals [pets] would be phased out."

Like PeTA, HSUS takes millions in donations each year but doesn't run a single shelter. Yet the group's rhetoric often seems more "moderate" than PeTA's. It does not talk about "phasing out" pets—only about reducing "pet overpopulation." The Summer 1991 issue of *HSUS News* quoted HSUS President John Hoyt as saying, "We shall, of course, continue to do battle against puppy mills."[8] HSUS's "Fact Sheet" defines a "puppy mill" as any "commercial breeding facility that mass produces dogs for resale in pet stores," no matter how well the animals are treated.[9]

Since 1990, HSUS and other groups, including the Peninsula

Humane Society, the Progressive Animal Welfare Society, and the Fund for Animals, have championed mandatory pet sterilization (and higher license fees to pay for it) from California to Maryland.

The purported rationale of such bans on breeding is to reduce the number of pets that need to be euthanized at shelters, often portrayed as a "pet-overpopulation crisis." Yet the American Humane Association (which *does* run shelters) reports that the number of animals euthanized at U.S. shelters dropped by 45 percent from 1980 to 1990.

In truth, there is no pet overpopulation problem. The Tufts Center for Animals and Public Policy has collected data about pet population that are striking:

CHANGES IN ANIMAL POPULATION[10]

	1973	1982	1990
U.S. Total Dogs and Cats (millions)	65	91	110
Dogs and Cats Euthanized (millions)	13	10	5
Percent of Animals Euthanized	20%	11%	4.5%

Since 1973 the number of pets has nearly doubled while the percent of animals euthanized has been cut by some three-quarters. In other words, the "pet overpopulation problem" declined even as the total pet population increased. Facts notwithstanding, animal rights agitation has grown more and more fanatical.

The hidden agenda is the extinction of all pets. As Wayne Pacelle of the Fund For Animals put it, "One generation and out. We have no problem with the extinction of domestic animals. They are creations of human selective breeding."[11]

Animal rights groups have succeeded in getting mandatory sterilization ordinances adopted in San Mateo County, California; King County, Washington; Montgomery County, Maryland; and in many other counties and localities.

A typical mandatory sterilization ordinance requires that all pet owners, including fanciers, have their animals spayed and neutered or pay a fee. Animal rights groups try to impose financial costs so heavy that fanciers will not be able to afford to breed animals. A predictable consequence of higher license fees, moreover, is that more people will abandon their pets, reversing the decline in euthanization. Of course, more abandoned pets means a better fundraising potential for animal rights groups.

Because animals that compete in shows are required by the rules of competition not to be spayed or neutered, fanciers are badly hurt by such legislation. Even if the rules should be changed to allow spayed animals to be shown, what's the point? The purpose of any animal show is breeding.

For all their moral pretensions, animal rights advocates are hypocritical when they support mandatory sterilization. Their core conviction is that a person has no right to control an animal. For example, animal rightists condemn people who give distemper shots to animals since this constitutes human control; the animals don't ask us to do it. And yet they advocate compulsory sterilization of animals although animals don't ask us to sterilize them. Logical? Or fanatical?

Forced spaying and neutering is blatantly inconsistent with animal rights philosophy. But animal rights advocates are willing to live with the hypocrisy because they believe that sterilization is a pragmatic way to achieve their ultimate goal, their "final solution"—to eliminate pets no matter what the cost to animals.

Animal rights propaganda likes to portray pet shop owners as being cruel to animals, "slave traders," to use their terminology. But nearly all pet store owners take excellent care of their animals. They understand the obvious: nobody will buy animals that are mistreated or malnourished. People who become pet shop owners love animals or they wouldn't be in that business in the first place.

Yet Mr. Hoyt of HSUS says: "The 'good' pet stores we shall encourage to become even better, which ultimately might mean selling no dogs or cats." Everything else is classified as "exotics," which Hoyt also wants to ban. In the meantime, he exhorts us: "Don't breed, don't buy, don't even accept giveaways."[12]

The New Jersey Animal Rights Alliance has stated, "In an ideal society where all exploitation and oppression has been eliminated, it will be NJARA's policy to oppose the keeping of animals as 'pets'."[13]

John Bryant explains how this is to be done: "The cat, like the dog, must disappear.... We should cut the domestic cat free from our dominance by neutering, neutering, and more neutering, until our pathetic version of the cat ceases to exist."[14]

A breed club magazine editor recently reported that animal rights protestors had released dogs at a show. PeTA's Newkirk, whose organization is dependent on donations from pet lovers, demanded that the editor "apologize and retract your statements."[15]

The editor wrote back: "I was there, and personally observed ... the behavior of the group which claimed PeTA affiliation.... [T]hey screamed loudly that they were PeTA members.... The Security folks reported several opened crates and loosed dogs, and these people claimed they had done it and were glad they did it."[16]

The animal rights movement lures people who love pets not only to provide financial assistance but also to engage in protest activities, such as picketing and organizing.

Animal rightists also claim they "rescue" animals that would otherwise die. But when it comes to rescuing animals, they have a terrible track record, as PeTA showed at Aspin Hill and the Fund For Animals did at the Black Beauty ranch.

In its case, PeTA soon learned that it takes more than moral posturing to care for animals. Instead of life, PeTA's animals found death. Eighteen rabbits confiscated from a class of students were killed.

Simultaneously, PeTA killed some fourteen roosters it had "rescued" from ritual sacrifice by members of the Santeria religion because, it explained, instead of getting along in the free-range yard at Aspin Hill, the roosters staged cockfights! Such behavior contradicts Ingrid Newkirk's effusions that under her stewardship, "the lion will lie down with the lamb." For those roosters, the penalty for acting naturally was death.

PeTA's failures aside, the concepts of "companion animals" and "rescuing" animals are not idiosyncratic points—philosophical fine tuning—but central to understanding the behavior of animal rights groups towards pets and pet owners. They consider owning companion animals a temporary expedient, to be eliminated on that great day when the animal rights view of the world prevails.

Ingrid Newkirk has made herself very clear on this subject. As she explains, if it were up to her, she would neither allow humans to breed animals nor pet shops to sell them. Companion animals are acceptable only so long as they are "refugees from the animal shelters and the streets." This condition is merely temporary, however: "as the surplus of cats and dogs (artificially engineered by centuries of forced breeding) declined, eventually companion animals would be phased out, and we would return to a more symbiotic relationship—enjoyment at a distance."[17]

Their own polls reveal that the average animal rights donor has five pets. In order to keep the money pouring in, these groups try—not always successfully—to hide their anti-pet position. But PeTA has said quite frankly, "In a perfect world, all other-than-human animals would be free of human interference, and dogs and cats would be part of the ecological scheme."[18]

In that world, animals that fall victim to predation, cannibalism, or road-kills would be lucky. For the others, death would be slow and painful—mange, parvo, distemper, heartworm, rabies, or starvation—with no veterinary, no anaesthesia, no care.

Those of us who really care about animals should not let ourselves be conned into funding groups that would impose such a "perfect world" on our pets.

7

FUR
You Should Be Ashamed Not to Wear Fur!

London Times, Dec. 21, 1988 — A series of fire bombings claimed by the Animal Liberation Front (ALF) burned department stores and businesses associated with the fur trade and animal experimentation—the largest single attack to date. In London, fires burned Harrod's and Selfridge's stores. Other fire bombs were found at the House of Fraser and the Fur Review Publishing Co. In Birmingham, a fire device was found at Rackham's department store. In Cardiff, Wales, fire burned Howell's menswear department. In Plymouth, fire largely destroyed Dingle's department store.

This wave of terrorism had its origins in a 1965 film, *Les Phoques de la Banquise,* by the Artek Film Company. The film showed men clubbing harp seal pups with hakapiks, bleeding them out, and skinning them. Like any graphic footage of slaughter, it showed the animals' bodies writhing in reflexive postmortem spasms.

But the film also showed a group of pups that had been struck and bled, then left on their bellies, not on their backs, to bleed out. Their eyes were open, as is the case in any animal killed by trauma. Pup voices were dubbed onto the scene, giving the impression that the pups were still alive and conscious, writhing in their own blood.

The most horrifying scene showed a man cutting a live, conscious seal with a knife, without having clubbed it first. In 1969, the Canadian House of Commons held hearings on the incident. The man in the film testified under oath that he had been hired by the film-makers to skin the live seal without first rendering it unconscious in order to make a dramatic point.[1]

The only "animal abuse" documented by this footage was perpe-trated by the filmmakers themselves. Yet this hoax was exploited by groups like International Fund for Animal Welfare and Greenpeace, with help from celebrities like Brigitte Bardot, to convince the public that seal hunting should be banned.

As a result of the prohibition of sealskin imports into the United States and European Community, the international market col-lapsed, causing dire economic hardship to the maritime people of the High North. Consequently, the harp seal population exploded from 1.5 million to over 4 million, depleting the stocks of capelin and other prey of cod to such an extent that cod stocks suffered, and in 1992 Canada placed a moratorium on cod fishing.

The attack on sealskin was a classic example of how wildlife management policy based on ideology rather than science causes disaster. But it was just an opening attack in the war on fur. Just as predators in the wild target the youngest or weakest in a herd, animal rights groups started with sealers, an isolated and politically powerless group. Now they are moving on.

Furs are simply animal hides which are tanned leaving the hair on. People have been wearing furs since time immemorial. Accord-ing to the Bible, Adam and Eve clothed themselves in fig leaves, but God clothed them in animal skins. Prehistoric men and women wore skins, and history records that the use of animal fur has been universal and continuous.

Fur trade was an important part of the economy of North Amer-ica as early as the seventeenth century. It was the first industry, and responsible for the settlement of Canada and much of what is now the United States. Fur products are deeply ingrained in the history of every culture, including the United States. Diplomat Benjamin Franklin arrived in France during the American Revolution wear-ing a fur hat, and such legendary American figures as Daniel Boone and Davy Crockett are often portrayed wearing fur clothes. They were aping the Native Americans, whose lives and cultures re-volved in large degree around hunting animals and wearing furs.

Today as in the past, furs are used for many purposes, most notably as clothing—coats, hats, collars, and linings for gloves and boots. People in particularly cold areas, such as northern Canada, Alaska, Russia, and Poland, depend on fur for their very survival.

The attack on fur usually focuses on trapping. People have used traps to catch animals for the past 25,000 years. Archeological finds have uncovered Paleolithic artwork portraying animal traps, with some evidence that the trap preceded the bow and arrow. From prehistoric times to the present, every continent shows evidence of traps that were used to catch animals, fish, and birds.

Today, trapping is typically a part-time occupation. Both European and aboriginal populations in Alaska and Canada rely on trapping as part of their subsistence as do residents of some areas of the contiguous United States, such as southern Louisiana, the Ozarks, and the eastern shore of Maryland.

Trappers have always led a difficult life, enduring bitter cold weather to get winter pelts. But today, the greatest difficulty they face is the political movement to outlaw their existence. It is a battle that pits Hollywood stars vs. backwoodsmen, urban vs. rural, rich vs. poor.

To attack the trappers, animal rights groups publish photographs of dead animals (often dogs or cats) caught in steel-jawed leghold traps with mangled and broken limbs. The photos are mostly fakes, featuring road-killed carcasses.

Animal rights activists exploit the old folk tales that a trapped animal will "gnaw off" its own limb to escape.

Predators like wolverines have traditionally raided northern trap lines for easy prey, leaving many an early trapper to find only a paw in the trap. The Wildlife Society, the association of professional wildlife biologists, reports that in fifty years of trapping and studying animals, it has found such cases to be extremely rare. Even lacerations and abrasions are the exception. Animal rights groups are well aware of these facts, but they continue to exploit the myth with slogans such as "Get a feel for fur—slam your hand in a car door."

On one occasion when I debated a representative of PeTA on a TV talk show in 1992, the PeTA spokeswoman reiterated the charge that trapping produces enormous suffering. I responded by setting a No. 2 steel-jaw leghold trap (the kind used to catch larger animals like coyotes) and catching my own hand in it. I held it up as refutation of her claim of "torture." It has not stopped PeTA from repeating its allegations.

A new padded-jaw (or "soft catch") trap is on the market. It is like a steel-jaw trap with rubber on the jaws. I have tried it but find that, at least on my hand, it hurts a little more than the regular trap, which causes a sting but certainly not major pain.

Animal rights groups often claim that animals are left in traps for days on end to die of starvation, disease, or exposure. But the law in almost every jurisdiction requires that traps be checked every 24–36 hours. Trappers make daily, early-morning checks, both to reduce losses to predators, and to minimize injury to trapped animals and their pelts.

Activists also claim that trappers indiscriminately trap pet dogs and cats, permanently maiming and crippling them. Again, simply not so. Not only do trappers have a humanitarian interest in avoiding trapping someone's pet, they have a clear economic interest as well. The amount of money a trapper earns depends on catching specific species, not anything that moves. If a pet is caught in a trap, that trap cannot then catch a furbearer, and the trapper gains nothing for his effort except the hostility of the pet owner. Consequently, trappers use specialized trap sets and lures that discourage nontarget species, such as dogs and cats.

If a nontarget animal is accidentally trapped, the leghold trap permits the trapper to release it unharmed. Where the leghold trap is banned, "instant kill" traps, such as the Conibear, must be used. So any pets accidentally trapped are finished.

The steel-jaw leghold trap is used for animal damage control by professional wildlife organizations (such as the Wildlife Society), conservation organizations (such as Ducks Unlimited, the Izaak Walton League, the National Audubon Society, and the National Wildlife Federation), and government agencies (such as the U.S. Fish and Wildlife Service and state wildlife agencies).

In the United States, most laws regulating trapping are enacted and applied at the state level. Laws regulating the kind of traps that can be used and the duration of trapping seasons have been passed in every state except Hawaii, which has no furbearing animals. Local laws also play a role, although to a more limited degree.

Relevant federal laws apply to interstate commerce, threatened or endangered species, species listed under international treaties, and trapping on federally owned lands. Other government regulations include seasons, licensing, zones, registered traplines, limits, quotas, and restrictions on traps and trapping techniques.

In the United States it is illegal to trade in the fur of any endangered species. Contrary to the claims of animal rights groups, no species is threatened by trapping today. Moreover, despite declining habitat, furbearer populations are larger and healthier than in the past, because of scientific wildlife management through trapping.

In Europe, however, animal rights groups have banned trapping in Germany and other countries. The result has been a population explosion among furbearers. Starvation, road-kills, cannibalism, mange, and rabies are now rampant throughout that continent. In 1990, ten people were bitten by rabid foxes in downtown Berlin alone. In France, five thousand people have to be treated for rabies exposure each year due to uncontrolled foxes.

In desperation, the European Parliament is debating a Europe-wide dog registry to check the spread of canine rabies. And the UK is installing grates on the new tunnel spanning the English Channel (the "Chunnel") to slow the migration of rabid animals from the continent.

In Canada, more than half the trappers are Native Americans. Indigenous Survival International reports that the attack on trapping has slashed the income of Native American tribes such as Aleuts, Inuits, and Metis by more than 60 percent, causing a wave of unemployment, alcoholism, and suicide. According to the *Toronto Star*, "a severe downturn in trapping has led to increasing suicides among aboriginal people."[2] In one small trapping community, twenty of the sixty teenagers attempted suicide, and nine succeeded.

Animal rights leaders are singularly unsympathetic to the plight of such animal-dependent cultures. Priscilla Feral of Friends of Animals (FoA), for example, was outraged in 1987 that American Aleuts were still permitted to hunt seals for food. "They're playing politics, knuckling under to the goddamn Aleuts," she said. "The Aleuts don't need to eat those seals."[3]

In the United States, animal radicals have stringently restricted trapping in Massachusetts, New Jersey, and Florida. Tom Krause, editor of *American Trapper Magazine*, reported that between 1986 and 1991, the number of active trappers fell from 500,000 to 100,000. Only 85,000 trappers are still actively working.[4]

The predictable result is record overpopulation of furbearers. Raccoons are causing millions of dollars of damage in crop depredation; beaver are stripping endangered trees and flooding forests; and coyotes and foxes are killing increasing numbers of livestock and pets from California to New York.

Nutria, a destructive furbearing species from South America (which are not endangered), escaped from captivity in the United States many years ago. They are now demolishing fragile wetlands from the Chesapeake Bay to the Mississippi Delta, destroying nesting habitat, and causing a population decline in many endangered shorebirds and sea turtles. According to Greg Linscombe, a Louisiana wildlife biologist, "They're eating the marshes right down to the mud."[5]

What is especially troubling to environmentalists is that Louisiana marshlands contain some of the richest wildlife habitats in North America. Thousands of these acres exist because of expensive water control structures. Muskrats and other aquatic furbearers create extensive damage to dikes, and trapping is the only effective method of keeping these populations in check.

When commercial trappers don't regulate the population of furbearers, government agents must do it at taxpayer expense. Wildlife agencies use traps to control such species, as well as the predators that kill endangered wildlife, livestock, and pets.

But animal rights groups *oppose* conservation—whether conducted by private organizations or by public authorities. PeTA, for example, condemns the use of tax dollars to help ranchers protect their livestock. A PeTA "Factsheet" comments: "These government hunters slaughter thousands of coyotes, mountain lions, bobcats, and other predators considered a threat by livestock ranchers, who often let their flocks and birds roam unattended on public lands that are part of many animals' habitat."[6]

When forest officials in San Bernadino, California, trapped a colony of beavers that had nearly leveled one of only two aspen groves in southern California in 1989, the *San Bernadino Sun* reported that PeTA spokesman Donna Ramsey said PeTA "totally opposes any trapping" and even opposed moving the beavers.[7]

Fur is a renewable, biodegradable, nonpolluting resource. This gives people an incentive to keep furbearer populations healthy and to protect their habitat. Yet animal rights groups advocate the use of "fake fur" as a substitute for fur—even though synthetic "furs" are petroleum products, the manufacture of which involves vinyl chloride and other deadly toxins. Pollution is a natural by-product of the manufacture of fake fur. The choice of fake fur is not environmentally responsible.

When Hollywood stars model imitation furs to show their dedication to protecting animals from people, they never think beyond their chic cause *de jour* from which they hope to get some good media exposure. Sadly, by not wearing real fur they not only harm the environment, they also hurt the very animals they claim to be saving. For example, a frightening result of the decline in trapping is the mid-Atlantic raccoon rabies epizootic (animal epidemic) that is spreading like wildfire. Rabies, a deadly disease of the nervous system, spreads rapidly when animals are overpopulated. It can, moreover, be transmitted between species and from animals to people.

Death by rabies is slow, agonizing torture for an animal, far worse than anything administered by man. More frightening, people and pets are now being attacked by rabid coyotes, foxes, raccoons, skunks, woodchucks, beaver, and even squirrels. A Canadian was recently bitten by a raccoon while watching a movie in a theater. But the raccoon's body was cremated by the Toronto Humane Society (which lobbied to ban trapping) before its brain tissue could be studied for the rabies virus, thus making it necessary for the human victim to undergo painful rabies shots. According to the *Toronto*

Sun, Dr. Ann Moon of the Toronto Public Health Service commented, "It seems that their concern for animal welfare and animal rights conflicts with our concern for human health."

Animal rights organizations ignore or deny the health consequences of their policies. If a child dies from rabies, it's just too bad. FoA pretends that wildlife rabies is insignificant, asserting: "Pet vaccination programs are the proven barrier between humans and any wildlife sickness outbreak, which left to its own devices, exhausts itself."[8] Unfortunately, while pet vaccinations do help, wildlife/human contact does occur and disease does spread. (Incidentally, pet vaccinations are the product of animal research.)

In 1990, FoA persuaded the town council of Cheltenham, Massachusetts, to ban trapping. Two years later, the local beaver had become so overpopulated that they contaminated two of the town's wells, threatening the local water supply. Outraged citizens demanded that the council repeal the ban, which it did, despite the protests of FoA. Once again, wildlife management policy based on ideology, rather than science, produced disaster.

Wild furbearers have extremely high natural rates of reproduction and mortality. Any surplus not harvested by man suffers and goes to waste. The vast majority dies within the first year of life from starvation, predation, exposure, hypothermia, or diseases such as mange, heartworm, tularemia, giardiasis, tapeworms, or distemper, which attacks the nervous system, causing blindness and painful death.

The choice is not between trappers killing animals or animals living long lives. Rather, it is between animals dying humanely or dying a slow, brutal death from other animals, starvation, or disease. *If it weren't for humans wearing furs, many species of furbearing animals would become extinct.*

Using wildlife for human benefit is an incentive to keep wildlife populations and the environment healthy. Lack of harvest has caused increased animal suffering, devastation of our environment, and threats to human life. The "compassionate" animal cult, with its millions of dollars, has not given a penny to fill the wildlife management gap created by its attack on trappers.

As Louisiana wildlife biologist Greg Linscombe put it: "If you're really concerned [about the environment], buy a fur coat."[9]

Animal groups oppose not just trapping but the use of fur itself. "We aren't interested in a more humane trap. We're interested in abolishing this [fur] industry altogether," says Victoria Miller, national coordinator of the Canadian group ARK II, which took over the Toronto Humane Society in 1986.[10] "We are only going to be satisfied with the destruction of the fur industry," agrees Wayne Pacelle, executive director of the Fund For Animals.

Trapping is a modest fraction of the fur industry, even though it is the showcase of the antifur movement. Of furs sold in the United States today, 80 percent are not trapped but raised on ranches. In addition to pelts, fur farmers harvest their animals for protein meal. Minks produce mink oil, an ingredient in hypoallergenic soaps, cosmetics, and hair care products. Even the mink manure, which is rich in nutrients, is used as a natural fertilizer for crop fields. These animals do not die "for the sake of vanity," as animal rights propaganda likes to put it.

The fur-farming industry in the United States began shortly after the Civil War. Since then, American fur farmers have been highly creative. They were the first to develop black mink, a color which is rare in nature.

In North America, most fur farms are family owned. The high economic investment ensures that furbearing animals are well cared for. They are bred prudently and given dietary supplements and veterinary attention.

Animal rightists complain about the fur farm cages that are constructed with wire bottoms, which they claim hurt the animals' feet. As usual this assertion has no basis in fact and is another example of anthropomorphism. They are projecting their feelings onto the animals. Extensive studies have demonstrated that the wire does not hurt their paws, which have very tough pads. Instead, these cages allow the animals' waste to fall through the wire floor and thus lessen the chance of disease.

Activists also claim that the cages are so small that they cause furbearers high stress. But recent scientific research in Denmark, using comparative biochemical sampling, has conclusively demonstrated that caged furbearers suffer no harm.

Finally, animal rightists assert that furbearers are tortured when they are killed. Such charges make for good fund-raising, but they are not true. The only methods of killing certified by the Fur Farm Animal Welfare Coalition are those approved by the American Veterinary Medical Association—pure carbon monoxide, dioxide bottled gas, or lethal injection—the same means used at animal shelters.

To use reason rather than emotion in considering the fur issue, let's start with a question: What's the moral difference between fur and leather? None. Indeed, the same theory that condemns fur also condemns leather, wool, down, and even silk.

So why do animal rightists single out fur? In the United States, 90 percent of fur coats are worn by women. (Animal rightists are prudent enough not to harass Hell's Angels bikers in leather jackets.)

But there is more to it than sexism and cowardice. Remember, the seal hunters were the first target because they were the smallest and politically weakest. Next came the trappers, and now the fur farmers and retailers. Leather workers, shepherds, and the rest are just down the line.

Meanwhile, ALF has declared war on trappers and anyone having business dealings with trapping. The danger involved can be seen from an article appearing in the extremist environmental publication *Earth First! Journal* that calls for "direct action." It urges ALF supporters to have "a quiet little party in the trappers' fur shed where they keep their traps, pelts, and assorted equipment."[11] It then provides instructions on how to sabotage mink farms, such as releasing the breeding stock and spraying the animals with dyes to ruin their pelts. Fur stores, it goes on, could be hurt by gluing the locks, spray painting the merchandise, and etching the windows.

The article lists specific targets, including furriers, trap and lure manufacturers, fur farms, fur salons, and even publications that support fur. Free speech joins private property in the ashcan.

But most people oppose the war on fur. In 1990 the people of Aspen, Colorado, rejected by nearly 2–1 a ballot proposal that would have banned the sale of wild animal furs there.

Intimidation is wrong, and, thankfully, it often doesn't work. Recently, a woman walked past an antifur protest wearing a fake fur jacket. A protestor, thinking her coat was real, splattered her with red paint. The owner of the coat sued the group sponsoring the protest, received a sizeable settlement, and used the money to buy her first real, beautiful, full-length fur.

8

ENTERTAINMENT AND RECREATION
Lights, Camera, Activism

Animal rights is not a typical protest movement. Not only are its ideas extremist, but its behavior goes beyond the bounds of decency and civility—not to mention legality. Consider just one example: animal rightists tried to destroy the life's work of an entertainer and to disgrace him publicly because they disapproved of using animals to entertain people.

In August 1989, animal rights activists released a videotape secretly filmed behind stage at the Stardust Hotel in Las Vegas. The film purported to show Bobby Berosini, a famous animal trainer, abusing the orangutans performing in his act.

According to PeTA, Ottavio Gesmundo, a dancer at the Stardust, made the films on his own in mid-July 1989 and sent the tapes to PeTA on July 17. Incredibly, by July 19–20—two or three days after the tapes were mailed from Nevada to PeTA's east coast location—PeTA had reviewed his data, located experts on primates, had them draft affidavits, obtained government documents on Berosini, and dispatched two staffers (authorized to retain attorneys and investigators) to Nevada.

The activists distributed their videotape to the media and it was shown on news and programs such as "Entertainment Tonight." Government authorities were called in to investigate. The Humane Society of Southern Nevada and the Society for the Prevention of Cruelty to Animals (which, according to local laws, have the power to investigate animal abuse charges) and the U.S. Department of Agriculture (USDA) (which is responsible for enforcing the Animal

Welfare Act) became involved in the case. The Humane Society took custody of the orangutans, with Berosini's consent, for sixty-three days.

Berosini charged that he had been set up by enemies in the Stardust Hotel show. He contended that as he and his handlers were preparing to go on stage, people unknown to him were taunting the orangutans, which aroused them.

After thorough investigations, the Humane Society and the Department of Agriculture concluded that there was no evidence of abuse by Berosini. The Humane Society added that the animals were in excellent condition.

Berosini filed suit against the animal rightists. PeTA filed a countersuit contending that the animals had been abused. After expert witnesses were allowed to examine the orangutans, the judge dismissed PeTA's countersuit.

The defendants in the Berosini suit included PeTA and its investigator, Jeanne Roush (who has since replaced Kim Stallwood as PeTA's executive director); the Performing Animal Welfare Society (PAWS) and its president Pat Derby; Ottavio Gesmundo, Seamus Brennan, and Simone Turner (alleged accomplices of Gesmundo); and Linda Levine (who distributed most of the videotapes).

The trial involved the testimony of thirty witnesses. On August 11, a jury dropped three of the individual defendants—Brennan, Turner, and Levine—and held the other defendants guilty of various combinations of:

(#1) invasion of privacy (unreasonable intrusion upon the seclusion of another)
(#2) invasion of privacy (appropriation of another's name and likeness)
(#3) defamation

After revision by the judge, the awards were as follows:

PeTA—#2 ($500,000) and #3 ($1,000,000)   Total $1,500,000
Roush—#2 ($250,000) and #3 ($500,000)   Total $ 750,000
Gesmundo—#1 ($250,000) and #3 ($500,000)   Total $ 750,000

PAWS—#3 ($50,000)
Derby—#3 ($50,000)

Grand Total = $3,100,000[1]

Berosini was delighted. "I won a victory," he said. "If they would have awarded me one dollar, I would have said, 'Thank you, God.' "[2]

In addition to the cash award, PeTA's attorneys were held in contempt and fined for introducing "manufactured" evidence. To destroy the career of an honest person, animal rightists were willing to falsify sworn evidence.

PeTA is appealing the judgment, and Putting People First has submitted an *amicus curiae* brief on behalf of Bobby Berosini.

Berosini was targeted not because of any purported "abuse," which is irrelevant to PeTA's ends, but as an example to all entertainers and, of course, as the impetus for a fund-raising drive.

Even after the jury voted unanimously that PeTA lied, PeTA used the verdicts to repeat the libel and raise more money. In the July/August 1990 issue of *PeTA News*, the organization urged its members to call the Stardust Hotel's toll free reservation number and "ask why the hotel continues to employ someone who has been videotaped beating animals. . . ."[3] The September/October issue informed members that the videotapes showed the performer repeatedly "beating and punching the animals" and again urged readers to "send a contribution to PeTA to help with PeTA's Berosini lawsuit."[4]

As for the trial, PeTA said the verdict was proof of corruption: "You can never win here. The casinos are too strong. . . ." And, of course, "Make a donation to help cover PeTA's legal fees."[5]

The Berosini case is not the only one to demonstrate the lengths the opposition to the use of animals in entertainment will go, no matter how well the animals are treated. Take rodeo, for example, a favorite target of animal rightists. Rodeos are an American phenomenon originating in the nineteenth-century West. The term is derived from the Spanish word "rodear," which means to round-up, and subsequently described a competition among cowboys in the demonstration of their skills. Today the most famous rodeo is Canada's annual Calgary Stampede.

To the world, the symbol of America is the cowboy, whose life revolved around animals. The rodeo is a tribute to him. Cowboys developed the West. They herded cattle across the country, worked on ranches and on the range roping, branding, and caring for livestock. These same skills are celebrated by rodeos.

Rodeos developed as cowboys from one ranch challenged those from another. These events became institutionalized through professional rodeo contests.

Today rodeo is a highly competitive sport. Rodeos generally consist of three bucking events in which a contestant tries to ride a bull or horse under specified conditions. The contestant is judged by how well he rides, the animal on how well it bucks, and the rider with the highest combined score wins. In addition, there are timed events—calf-roping, steer-wrestling, team-roping, and barrel-racing. Few people know that rodeo ranks as the No. 1 spectator sport in the United States.

Special junior rodeos are springing up all over the United States. In 1961, the National Little Britches Rodeo Association was organized and patterned along the guidelines set up by the Professional Rodeo Cowboys Association (PRCA). It sanctions more than a hundred rodeos each year in the United States in which nearly 14,000 contestants between the ages of eight and seventeen participate.

Rodeos are good not only for their entertainment value but for the care taken of the animals. Rodeo animals constitute a costly investment. If rodeo performers were to abuse their animals they would be throwing money away. But they also love them—the pampered horses and steers attest to that. Rodeo livestock are well fed, are often given special vitamin injections, and are regularly dewormed. In return most animals perform for only seconds or a few minutes during a performance.[6]

In their war on rodeos, animal rightists propagate any story that comes in handy. One of their handouts has a caption reading,

"Cruelty—Not Sport." It adds: "Today's professional rodeo cow-boys don't make their living on the range—they make it in the arena where horses, calves, and bulls are roped, pushed, kicked, and shocked, and otherwise abused to entertain the crowd and help a cowboy make a buck."[7]

Animal rightists focus their attack on the flank strap, electric prod, and calf-roping. A flank strap is a belt that fits an animal across the abdomen the way a belt fits human beings. It's not across the genitals, as animal rightists claim (virtually all bucking horses are in fact mares and geldings, so they don't have the necessary physical equipment), and the strap does not harm the animal.[8] Since the device is unfamiliar to the animal, the horse or bull tries to kick out of it. In so doing, the animal kicks higher with its back legs. The more the animal bucks, the looser the flank strap becomes.

An electric prod is touched to the bucking animal seconds before an event starts. The prod induces a minor stimulus, but does not cause pain.[9] The little buzz startles the animal to perform better, more like a "joy buzzer" than the electric chair animal rightists compare it with.

Animal rightists dare contend that the electric prod is applied brutally into the rectum of horses and bulls to make them buck. The prod does no such thing; it surprises, rather than injures, animals; it is powered by the same small size "C" batteries that are used in flashlights.

Animal rightists also speak of the danger of killing or injuring calves when cowboys rope them. Cowboys often rope calves on the open range when the animals are sick, injured, or need branding. The method is quick and prevents the animal from injuring itself or the cowboy.

Very few calves are injured in rodeos, in part because competition calves weigh from 225 to 300 pounds. The animal injury rate at rodeos for animals is less than one-half of 1 percent, a much lower percent than injured cowboys.

The rodeos that are governed by professional rules and supervision, such as those of the International Professional Rodeo Association (IPRA), impose strict guidelines to protect animals.[10]

Not mentioned by the animal rightists, moreover, is the fact that many charities—including animal welfare organizations—use rodeos as fund raisers.

The bottom line, of course, is that animal rightists want to do away with rodeos. They show no interest in preserving a rich American heritage. They do not care about the economic harm done were rodeos to be abolished.

The same goes for circuses. Activists attend circuses around the country, dressed as clowns or other circus performers, and hand out to the children of unsuspecting parents propaganda-filled coloring books from PeTA and PAWS. Circuses too must go.

Animal acts in circuses predate ancient Rome, entertaining young and old alike. Since the days of P.T. Barnum, the circus in America has meant a procession of animals, trainers, clowns, and acrobats from the train station to the Big Top.

Circus people work with animals and care for them better than most people are cared for today. For animals to perform, they must be encouraged and rewarded, not mistreated. Trainers use the carrot—not the stick.

Circus people also look after their animals because trained animals are a major economic investment. Some cost hundreds of thousands of dollars. It makes no sense for circus people to abuse or neglect such a costly investment.

Take lions. Writer Vicki Hearne notes that in Africa, 75 percent of the lion cubs do not survive to the age of two. Those who do die at an average age of ten.[11] Lions in zoos and circuses live much longer. Asali, the movie and television lioness, was still working at age twenty-one. Wild orangutans in Borneo and Malaysia have a life expectancy of thirty-five years as opposed to fifty years in captivity.

In the course of a week, the animals may perform for fifteen or thirty minutes per day, sometimes even less. And for this easy effort, they eat regular well-balanced meals, are tended by veterinarians, exercise frequently, and are kept clean. Contrary to the horror stories of animal rights, when circus animals are transported, their trainers and caretakers take special care of the animals.

At the American Association of Zookeepers 1991 annual convention, a PeTA representative showed a videotape of an elephant being loaded into a boxcar. As the elephant disappeared into the car, a sudden gush of fluid trickled down the loading ramp. The PeTA representative claimed that the fluid was blood, evidence that the elephant handlers were cruelly beating the animal.

Unfortunately for PeTA, the elephant manager in charge of that move was present. He showed that PeTA's version of the story was pure fabrication. Elephants' legs are normally shackled in a car to prevent injury, he said, but before the shackles could be fastened this time, the elephant had stepped on one of them, slightly injuring one foot. The elephant then urinated, and this stream of urine, mingled with a little blood from the foot, was what PeTA had identified as a "gush" of blood. Had PeTA been right, he pointed out, that elephant would have died from blood loss.

The PeTA spokesperson was forced to back down. Yet PeTA later used this same video to convince the City Council of Toronto, Canada, to ban the circus there. That time, no experts were present to tell the truth. The cost to the community was estimated at $12 million.

For many people—especially urban children—circuses offer a rare opportunity to see live, exotic animals. There is no greater joy for a child than to see "The Greatest Show on Earth." And they help people to love, respect, and appreciate animals for what they are and for what they can do—not for the false anthropomorphic characteristics ascribed to them and artificially imposed in cartoons.

Like other forms of popular entertainment in the United States, circuses create jobs. Circuses help localities, too. They pay for advertisements in local newspapers and magazines, hire local security employees, order food and supplies from local merchants, and much besides.

In January 1991, city commissioners of Hollywood, Florida, barred the Great American Circus, an organization based in Sarasota, Florida, from exhibiting its elephants, lions, tigers, and chimpanzees at the Water Kingdom Amusement Park, scheduled for the following month.[12] The commissioners said that their move would serve as a warning that circuses were not welcome in the city unless their shows were limited to domestic and farm animal acts. The circus is sponsored by the Kiwanis Club of Hollywood and is one of its largest fund-raising programs for needy children.

Even more significant, perhaps, circuses are important for breeding rare and endangered species. They provide breeding animals for zoos and for reintroduction into the wild.

Then there are the zoos. Animal activists stage terrible attacks on zoos. At the San Diego Zoo in 1989, employees had their vehicles vandalized and tires slashed, and received numerous death threats. Despite such attacks, more Americans visit zoos and aquariums every year than attend sports events.

People can see a greater variety of animals at zoos than anywhere else. Not only do visitors observe animals, but they learn about them, too. To encourage people to be concerned about animals, zoos and aquariums have educational programs for the community. Schoolchildren love to go and learn about the lives of the different animals. Many youngsters are stimulated to such an extent that they decide to pursue careers involving the care or study of wildlife. Many zoologists, biologists, naturalists, conservationists, and veterinarians developed their interest in animals from their childhood visits to the zoo.[13]

Attention to the plight of animals and marine life is also important. Zoos and aquariums offer a safe haven where threatened species can be preserved and increased in numbers. Even when they can avoid predators, animals in nature often die because their food or water supply disappears. Zoos are crucial to captive breeding of endangered species.

Consider the Royal Bengal tigers. Gary G. Clarke, director of the Topeka Zoological Park, describes what life for the pair of Royal Bengal tigers in the Topeka, Kansas, zoo would be like if the animals were brought to the wilds of India:

They would be subject to natural disasters, diseases, parasites; they would have to protect and defend their territory at all times; they would never know where their next meal is coming from; they may be even hunted by man for their skin, or as a trophy to hang on a wall.[14]

In contrast, Clarke describes the life of tigers in the zoo:

But in the zoo, they have comfort, security, freedom from enemies, a balanced diet, veterinary attention, and room service every day. The fact that animals in zoos reproduce and raise their young, the fact that they live much longer than their counterparts in the wild, indicates they are adjusted to life in the zoo.[15]

Zoos have a remarkable record in preserving endangered species. The London Zoo has bred the rare Pere David's deer of China and reintroduced them to their native habitats. The San Diego Zoo is home to 150 species on the endangered list and has returned a dozen of them to the wild. Because of the National Zoo's work with golden lion tamarins, along with the cooperation of many other zoos, that species is being successfully reintroduced into the wild in Brazil. Other captive species that zoos have returned into the wild include the scimitar-horned oryx, thick-billed parrot, red wolf, and Arabian oryx; other species, like the Mongolian Wild Horse, are being prepared for reentry into the wild.

One of the most remarkable feats is being accomplished by two California zoos which are bringing back the California condor, a fabulous bird because of its great size and prehistoric ancestry. The California condors existed in the late Pleistocene age in much of North America, but they suffered a major decline about ten thousand years ago; by early 1983, the population had declined to about twenty-two birds, three of which were in captivity. Soon all that could be trapped were placed in captive breeding programs at the Los Angeles Zoo and the San Diego Wild Animal Park.

By mid-summer 1991, the total California condor population had reached fifty-three. The captive population had met the established criteria for freeing the birds in safe areas. According to Lloyd Kiff, curator of Ornithology at the Natural History Museum, the California condor program has been the "flagship of endangered species programs. . . . It generates a multitude of side benefits, including the development of new techniques for captive breeding, releases, and genetic analyses, as well as land preservation."[16]

Such recoveries and reintroductions would be impossible without zoos. But animal rightists are opposed to programs like condor reintroduction because, in their view, humans have no right to control animals. If they had their way, the California condor would have become a permanently lost national treasure.

It is sometimes said by well-meaning but uninformed people that zoo animals would be happier if they were able to "return" to their native homes. But today, about 80 percent of mammals displayed in North American zoological institutions are captive born, and 50 percent of these are offspring of captive-born parents.

Since most animals are not captured in the wild, the notion that if not for selfish humans, zoo animals would be roaming wild, free, and happy in the great outdoors is a myth. The reality is that if not for zoos, most of the animals in the zoos would not exist at all.[17]

Animal rightists have especially targeted dolphins and porpoises. At aquariums and theme parks, they have protested the display of these mammals and have tried to prevent the U.S. navy from using dolphins as an intelligence resource for national security.

They have destroyed vehicles and slashed tires at Sea World in San Diego, picketed researchers on whale diseases at Woods Hole, and attacked the New England Aquarium, claiming that one of its dolphins, Kama, was "violently ripped from the bosom of his family in the sea," when in fact Kama was born at Sea World.[18] The New England Aquarium is suing for defamation. If these people succeed in shutting down such aquariums, whales that are stranded on beaches around the country will no longer benefit from the marine mammal rehabilitation programs of these aquariums. And that is only one example.

As in many countries, zoos and aquariums in the United States are professionally run and abide by the highest standards. To be sure, a handful violate Animal Welfare Act guidelines, which is why the U.S. Department of Agriculture enforces compliance.

One major exception to the normally high standard of care is PeTA, whose Aspin Hill "sanctuary" was cited by the UDSA as an unlicensed animal exhibitor, operating in violation of the Animal Welfare Act, after it was caught killing healthy "rescued" animals in 1991 (see chapter 3).

The argument for horse-drawn carriage rides is simple—people enjoy them. One of the joys of visiting New York City is taking a carriage ride through Central Park.

As with other performing animals, horses in the carriage industry are treated very well by their owners and handlers. To mistreat a horse with overwork, inadequate feeding, or bad sanitary conditions would affect the animal's ability to work. The owner of a carriage business would have to be irrational or depraved to allow his animals to be abused.

Municipal ordinances, moreover, impose restrictions on the use of carriage animals, such as the proper temperature and hours of work, and government inspection assures that the animals are well cared for.

But in their continuing totalitarian campaign, animal rights extremists want to eliminate the carriage trade. They complain that the horses are badly treated and work on dangerous streets.

In 1989, in response to a campaign by the Carriage Horse Action Committee, an animal rights group, New York City adopted tough regulations on the proper area, hours, and temperature concerning the work of carriage horses. In the same year, because of pressure from the American Horse Protection Association and other such groups, the city of Venice, Florida, banned carriage horses altogether.

Animal rights activists in New York City have been trying for years to ban horse-drawn carriages, but without success. One activist was arrested in 1990 for assaulting a female carriage driver with mace.[19]

The public does not buy the attack on carriage horses. In November 1991, PeTA tried to ban horse-drawn carriages in Washington, D.C., and spent more than $100,000 on the initiative.[20] PeTA's campaign included hiring a local political consulting team and sending newsletters to thousands of homes in the District of Columbia.

Sarah Davies, the only remaining carriage operator in the District, spent $1,500 opposing the referendum. Putting People First weighed in too, with speeches, literature, and poll watching. We spent all of $300 when our copy machine broke down. A deciding event was captured by the TV news programs—two petite female carriage drivers substituted for the horses and pulled a carriage. It adequately debunked PeTA's contention that the task was impossibly arduous. In spite of the massive spending by PeTA, the referendum was overwhelmingly defeated by a vote of 62 to 38 percent—a victory of people over money.

Finally, let us turn to animal racing, one of the oldest and most popular sports in the world.

As long as man and animals have lived in symbiosis, they have cooperated in hunting. The animals have benefitted from the use of man's reason, while people have benefitted from the animals' superior speed, strength, endurance, and senses, such as scent.

The most important animal allies in our hunting heritage have been the dog and the horse. Both have produced specialized working breeds with superlative speed, the greyhound and the thoroughbred.

The selective breeding responsible for the development of such breeds was made possible by racing.

Greyhound racing has been labelled particularly inhumane by animal rights groups. Since ancient times, live rabbits have been used as lures to induce the animals to run. Animal rightists still complain about this practice, although in the United States, live lures were replaced with mechanical "rabbits" years ago. They also claim that racing dogs are routinely neglected or abused, and that animals no longer able to race are brutally killed.

In fact, the best racing dogs are actually retired early for breeding stock. The others were traditionally sold to processing companies to be rendered into commercial products, just like pigs, cattle, and other animals. Graphic descriptions of such uses of species commonly thought of as pets are exploited by animal rightists to provoke an emotional response.

But legitimate animal welfare groups, in cooperation with greyhound breeders, have recently started successful programs to adopt retired racing dogs to work on farms or become pets. The fact that these dogs make such good, although energetic, pets is evidence that they are not abused or neglected, as the animal rightists claim. Mistreated animals make terrible pets.

Racing greyhounds, like thoroughbred horses, must be well cared for if they are going to compete successfully. Their owners go to considerable expense to insure that they receive a nutritious diet and proper veterinary care. Otherwise, their more conscientious competitors drive them out of business.

Dog racing makes a better target than horse racing, simply because it is less popular than "the sport of kings." In the United States, more than 70 million people attend horse races each year, generating as many as 80,000 jobs and over $600 million in tax revenue. Even an animal-rights booster such as actress Loretta Swit enjoys the steeplechase, an event animal rights groups single out as especially "abusive." So much for consistency.

The attack on animal races is just as specious as the rest of the animal rights agenda. Thanks to racing, there is an incentive to bring beautiful, swift animals into the world, and to provide for their optimum health and well-being.

What should we call people who would take circuses away from kids and deprive them of a joyous occasion, shut down zoos and let endangered species disappear, destroy rodeos and end a valuable American tradition, abolish carriage rides and diminish romance, and stop horse and dog races and deny people the thrill of a sport? We could call them mean-spirited, silly, crazy, and maybe something worse. Whatever our choice, we can safely rule out "ethical."

9

HUNTING
The Virtue of Hunting

Greenpeace activist Graham Hood was arrested in 1992 for shooting at a hunter from a forest ranger's tower near Red Earth, Alberta, Canada.

This may be an extreme example of "hunter harassment," but it is a predictable result of animal rights propaganda labeling hunters as "murderers." Animal rightists take advantage of the unfamiliarity that the overwhelming majority of Americans have with life in the wild. In 1880, half of all Americans lived on farms and had a close association with animals and hunting. Today, only one in fifty lives on a farm. Consequently, most Americans learn about farming and hunting from such image makers as films and television.

This has enormous consequence for our story. Because *the less people know about animals from their own experience, the more likely they are to believe animal rights propaganda.* That is why the core of animal rights strength is in cities, where people are most removed from nature. As Richard Conniff keenly observed in an article in *Audubon Magazine*, "The [animal rights] movement has elevated ignorance about the natural world almost to the level of a philosophical principle."[1]

Animal rights policies have caused suffering and even death, not only to the animals they profess to love, but to people as well. As we shall see, wildlife management policies that are not in accord with scientific fact have tragic consequences.

We can do nothing about the problems animal rightists have already caused to hunting. But we should at least understand the

111

basic facts about hunting and wildlife and thus avert further damage to both humans and animals.

Contrary to the claims of animal rightists, people are not natural herbivores. Like some animals, such as crows and raccoons, we are omnivores, designed to eat both plants and animals. People have canine teeth, a mark of meat-eating species. And we are dependent on meat, eggs, and dairy products for our high-quality protein and vitamin B_{12}. Like most meat-eating species, moreover, people are predators. Our eyes face forward (like an owl or cat) rather than sideways (like a pigeon or rabbit).

Man has hunted from time immemorial. The earliest cave paintings at Lascaux and Altamira depict people hunting. As Aldo Leopold, "the father of conservation," wrote in *A Sand Country Almanac*, "The instinct that finds delight in the sight and pursuit of game is bred into the very fiber of the race."[2] In his *Meditations on Hunting*[3], philosopher José Ortega y Gasset concurred, as did George Santayana in his essay, "Why I Hunt."

Every culture, civilization, age, and continent shows evidence of hunting. Hunting binds people from prehistoric to contemporary societies.

For centuries Americans have hunted, and Native Americans before them. The Founding Fathers hunted. The pioneers who conquered our Western frontier hunted, as did such presidents as Abraham Lincoln, Theodore Roosevelt, Dwight Eisenhower, Jimmy Carter, and George Bush.

If most Americans are unfamiliar with hunting today, it is because they have moved away from their heritage. In colonial times, when Americans needed meat, they hunted for it. Today, most Americans hunt for meat in the supermarket. Where human eyes used to target live animals in motion, they now focus on the polyethylene package containing meat with the least trim and the right texture. Where seekers of food used to haul rifles or bows and arrows, their modern counterparts push shopping carts.

Animal rightists claim that hunters hunt just to kill, that they do not eat their prey. Rubbish. Americans eat more than 750 million pounds of game each year—roughly equivalent to 2 million beef cattle with an annual value exceeding $1.3 billion. People who rely on hunting for sustenance live in rural areas and are often poor. If they did not get a deer or other wild animal through hunting, they might have no meat at all.

To Native Americans, such as the Aleuts in Alaska and the Inuits and Metis in Canada, hunting is often not only a matter of sustenance but an element of their tradition and culture. Hunting cultures also include sealers and whalers in Newfoundland, Greenland, Iceland, Norway, and the Faroe Islands.

Most Americans who hunt are sportsmen. Sportsmen hunt animals as a source of food for their families, friends, or even for charities, like the Hunters for the Hungry program. Some big game hunters also hunt animals as trophies. But most sportsmen hunt for the total experience of being a part of nature and to put meat on their tables.

The hunting community also includes representatives of government agencies and conservation organizations. Wildlife management specialists hunt in order to regulate the population of particular species of animals. Professional wildlife biologists prescribe seasons, bag limits, and the number of licenses to control disease, crop depredation, overgrazing, overbrowsing, and soil erosion.

Animal rightists claim that hunters in the United States are a threat to endangered species. This is ludicrous. No species has ever been endangered by legal sport hunting. Uncontrolled market hunting was one factor in the demise of the passenger pigeon but there were other contributing factors—the deforestation of the eastern United States and, probably, eastern equine encephalitis. The buffalo was brought to the edge of extinction by a government bounty designed to destroy the Plains Indians' economy, an abhorrent example of Putting People Last.

It is a little known fact that the conservation movement owes much to hunters. At the end of the nineteenth century, U.S. hunters led the opposition to commercial killing of waterfowl and other birds, as well as to market hunting of numerous species of deer.

Teddy Roosevelt, the famed hunter and conservationist, started the Boone and Crockett Club, which helped hunters to lease or buy land for conservation, and hired biologists to do research on the ecology. The club was responsible for developing the classical theory of wildlife management. Where is the animal rightists' contribution?

American hunters have successfully lobbied for federal and international conservation regulation. Thanks to their efforts, in 1916 the United States and Great Britain entered into the Migratory Bird Treaty. In 1918, the Migratory Bird Treaty Act authorized the acquisition of land and water areas to establish sanctuaries for migratory birds. And in 1934, at the request of hunters, Congress passed the Migratory Bird Hunting Stamp Act, which required hunters to purchase a stamp (the "duck stamp") in order to hunt ducks, the proceeds from which were designated for new waterfowl refuge areas.

The Federal Aid in Wildlife Restoration Act of 1937 (or Pittman-Robertson Act) placed an 11 percent tax on the sale of hunting equipment. This revenue is used by both federal and state government wildlife agencies specifically to fund wildlife habitat, wildlife research, and other wildlife-related items. It has so far raised nearly $6 billion. Hunters lobbied for the bill, and they pay the tax. Where is the animal rightists' contribution?

The conservation legacy did not stop there. A 1986 treaty between the United States and Canada called for both countries to save wetlands and the migratory waterfowl that depended on them.

Hunters rely on their own initiatives as well. For example, Ducks Unlimited, a sportsmen's organization, began in the 1930s when drought threatened duck populations. Since then, the organization has collected and spent over $300 million to conserve and create wetland habitat in North America. It is the largest nonprofit, private-sector waterfowl conservation organization in the world and now works on three continents.

Hunters are active in preserving endangered or threatened species too. In 1900, Congress enacted the Lacey Act, designed to protect the bison from extinction; today, it is responsible for reducing the amount of illegal killing of wildlife.

Perhaps the most important legislation is the Endangered Species

Act (ESA). Under this law animals, birds, or fish designated as endangered or threatened are given federal protection. Though well intentioned, the law has recently become a battleground between conservationists and preservationists, with the latter using it as a weapon to attack property rights. Putting People First is working to amend the ESA to force the government to take human costs into account when it considers "listing" an animal.

Finally, American hunters are bound by international treaties and by laws at the national, state, and local levels. Virtually all conservation law has been drafted and supported by hunters.

Today, American hunters privately own or lease 250 million acres for conservation—roughly equivalent to the combined areas of Texas, New York, Illinois, and South Carolina! Hunters (7 percent of Americans) voluntarily pay for 75 percent of all state wildlife programs. All told, hunters pay over $619 million for government wildlife and habitat conservation each year. Where is the animal rightists' contribution?

Animal rightists claim that public lands are managed for hunting to the detriment of nonhunted species. Another wild charge. Of more than 1,150 species of birds and mammals found in the United States today, only 145 (12.5 percent) are legal game for recreational hunters.

Moreover, because state wildlife agencies spend only about 30 percent of their budgets on managing huntable wildlife, hunters (7 percent of the population) provide 45 percent of the funding to manage wildlife species that are not hunted. Where is the animal rightists' contribution?

Under the guidance of professional wildlife biologists, sportsmen now regulate wildlife populations, preventing the disease, environmental degradation, and crop depredation that result from wildlife overpopulation. As a result, the United States today has the largest, healthiest wildlife populations in the world, and many species once threatened by extinction, including the pronghorn antelope, wood duck, white-tailed deer, and wild turkey, have been restored to abundance.

In contrast, animal rights groups do *nothing* for wildlife habitat conservation. On the contrary, they interfere in wildlife management, obstruct veterinary research, and oppose the captive breeding of endangered species.

Despite the good that hunters do, animal rights advocates demand "the total abolition of sport hunting." Their war is being fought on many battlefields, including government (laws, regulations, and judicial proceedings), the mass media (television and newspaper propaganda), and the hunting preserves themselves.

Concerning hunters, the animal rightists' tactics become ugly. They harass the hunters personally, puncture hunters' tires, and spread poisoned baits for hunting dogs—this from the "be kind to animals" crowd. The activists have also shot arrows into livestock and road-killed deer as part of their attempts to smear the image of hunters.

They seem to forget that in the United States some of the nation's leading conservationists and naturalists were hunters—Henry David Thoreau, John James Audubon, "Ding" Darling, George Grinnell, and Ernest Thompson Seton. It was the hunter Gifford Pinchot who coined the word conservation.

Today, hunters are members of the boards of directors of major conservation associations, including the National Audubon Society, the Nature Conservancy, the National Wildlife Federation, the Izaak Walton League, the Boone and Crockett Club, and Ducks Unlimited.

But animal rightists prefer to ignore hunters' contributions to conservation and play on the emotions by evoking the image of "cute" species. Typical of this is a 1990 fund-raising letter from the Committee to Abolish Sport Hunting, which tells readers, "Bambi and Yogi the Bear are counting on you."[4]

No film has done more to misrepresent deer than the Walt Disney film *Bambi*. In this cartoon classic, the fawn Bambi loses its mother to evil hunters; there are no predators, starvation, disease, or road-kills. Nature is without death or tragedy—except for hunters.

In short, the film ignores the facts of life. Consider Catoctin Mountain Park in Maryland, the home of Camp David, the presidential retreat. The Secret Service prohibits hunting in the park, so the population of deer hit 400–800 by 1991. Its carrying capacity is 125–175 deer.

The deer have damaged Catoctin's vegetation and wildlife, stripping flora to a height of six feet and causing uncontrollable erosion. According to a study by wildlife scientists Robert J. Warren and Charles R. Ford of the University of Georgia, the overabundance of deer could eventually destroy the forested ecosystem of the park.[5]

These deer do not respect "No Trespassing" signs, as they have wandered into private property, destroying farm crops. Large numbers of deer have died from disease and starvation. Similar problems have been found in twenty of the other national parks, mostly in the eastern regions of the United States.

Animal rightists, of course, are among the leading defenders of the deer. The HSUS opposed thinning Catoctin's deer herd, despite the views of wildlife specialists.

Overpopulated deer and elk resort to eating hay, thistles, stems, and twigs. These cause penetrating wounds of the mouth, which permit intestinal flora to gain entry to the animal's bloodstream. The animals' *fusobacterium necrophorum* becomes a deadly pathogen once it enters the animal's bloodstream, causing necrotic stomatitis or necrobacillosis, along with a variety of other diseases. Poorly nourished populations suffering from protein deficiency lack antibodies to fight the infection, producing a slow and agonizing death.

When overpopulated buffalo migrated out of Yellowstone Park in their quest for food in the 1980s, they moved into ranch lands and posed a direct threat to the food supply of cattle. Bison also threatened the cattle with brucellosis, a disease that causes pregnant female cattle to abort. If a domestic cow gets the disease, laws require a rancher to quarantine his entire herd.

As might be expected, animal rightists were hostile to the ranchers and wanted to prevent the buffalo from being controlled. Wayne Pacelle, national director of Fund For Animals, made the glib assertion that "credible wildlife scientists [he named not one] argue that Yellowstone's brucellosis strain may not even be potentially transmissible to cattle."[6]

Recognizing the danger to livestock, Montana wildlife officials allowed hunters to kill the escaping buffaloes. Animal rightists immediately jumped in, showed pictures of hunters shooting the animals, and through sheer emotionalism managed to end the hunt—in a state in which half the adult men and one in five women hunt.

Animal rightists also try to undermine hunting by using popular prejudice as a weapon of class warfare. They attack fox hunting, for example, by charging that it is a sport in which the wealthy get their thrills through killing or torturing animals.

But don't be fooled. Animal rightists hate the rest of us just as much. They label hunters as "rednecks," "Bubbas," and "Neanderthals," whom they regard as boorish, low-class, beer-swilling slobs who delight in killing.[7]

Animal rights advocates suggest controlling prey populations by reintroducing large predators, such as wolves, mountain lions, or black bears, near population centers. But such predators maul or kill children and adults as well. In India, where hunting has been outlawed since 1972, an estimated 150 children are killed by Bengal tigers each year. There, forest rangers carry weapons not to protect themselves from animals, but to escape being lynched by outraged villagers.

Since animal rightists believe that animals have the same rights as humans, they also oppose scientific wildlife management. According to Daniel J. Decker and Tommy L. Brown, two scholars in the Department of Natural Resources at Cornell University, "Some wildlife management professionals believe that the animal rights movement is one of the greatest threats to wildlife conservation faced by the profession."[8]

Animal rightists are the real enemies of conservation and the environment. Two recent cases illustrate the point: When the Sierra Club supported a U.S. Fish and Wildlife Service program to trap and kill non-native red foxes that were preying on two endangered bird species, the Animal Lovers Volunteer Association brought suit in court. When the National Audubon Society endorsed a Bureau of Land Management decision to poison ravens that were killing the endangered desert tortoise in the Mojave Desert, HSUS sued and the program was stopped.[9] With friends like animal rightists, environmentalists don't need enemies.

In 1972, Princeton became the first town in New Jersey to ban hunting with firearms. As might be expected, the number of deer in Princeton exploded from two hundred in 1972 to 1,200 by 1990. In 1990, nearly two hundred deer died in car collisions in Princeton, and people complained about deer destroying their gardens and about the spread of Lyme disease carried by deer ticks. (Lyme disease attacks the central nervous system and inflames brain tissue. In its later stages, the disease can be incurable and deadly.)

Officials at the Institute of Advanced Study at Princeton felt they had to do something about the deer on their 640 acres of wooded land and decided to have an annual bow and arrow hunt. "It causes some controversy and debate," said Allen I. Rowe, associate director of the institute. "People say it's cruel. But what are we going to do—put timber wolves in the woods?"[10]

At a recent Texas antihunting protest, the Fund For Animals (FFA) displayed a cardboard cutout of baseball star and bowhunter Nolan Ryan with an arrow through his crotch. When Putting People First publicized a video of the incident by Texas Sportsmen's Legal Defense Fund (TSLDF), FFA claimed the demonstrator targeting Ryan was an agent provocateur. So the TSLDF offered a reward for the unknown woman's identity. Sure enough, the person turned out to be a well-known local animal rights activist. And standing on the other side of the Ryan cutout was Ingrid Newkirk, national director of PeTA!

When forced to deal with the reality of problems caused by wildlife overpopulation, animal rightists propose ludicrous solutions that could never work, such as fencing and oral contraceptives. It would be impossible to fence nature trails, campgrounds, parks, and playgrounds. And while the development of oral contraceptives may be useful in a few isolated instances, to discover which cases those are would require animal research, which the animal rightists oppose. Alternatively, there are too many animals for contraceptives to be injected successfully.

The ultimate irony is that the very same animal rightists who say we humans have no right to infringe on animals—to take milk from cows or wool from sheep—insist that it is all right for humans to deny the animals their reproductive freedom.

Advocates of animal rights sometimes talk of relocating animals to solve overpopulation. But most relocated animals die as a result of stress—and the death is not pleasant.[11]

Animal rightists suggest that humans wear "protective clothing" when faced with health hazards from diseased animals; they have other equally ludicrous proposals. Their solution for the protection of animals, as one writer notes satirically, is that "people should live in cages so animals can be free to roam."[12]

In another attempt to frighten nonhunters, animal rightists play up hunting accidents. But due to hunter safety training classes begun in 1946, the hunting accident rate has been reduced by 50 percent nationwide. A nonhunter is twenty times as likely to die from bee, wasp, or hornet stings as from wounding by a hunter.

The animal rights opposition to hunting is not really based on concern for animal welfare, conservation, or public safety. These are smokescreens to mask the true motivation: the ideology that believes—in the words of Walter Simpson, of Animal Rights Advocates of Western New York—"that hunting is a sick, macho act taken to an extreme."[13] Hunting, in reality, is important to the well-being of both people and animals.

Opposition to hunting is irresponsible and perverse. The choice is not between animals being hunted or living in Bambi-like bliss, but between scientifically regulated sustainable use and catastrophe. By monitoring nature and the environment, hunters prove they are the true friends of animals.

PART THREE

DANGER AND OPPORTUNITY: THE THREAT TO HUMAN RIGHTS AND HOW TO FIGHT BACK

10

THE DANGER OF ANIMAL RIGHTS
Ideas Have Consequences

It is hard to overestimate the danger posed by a fanatical commitment to the ideology of animal rights. As these pages have shown, it harms our economy, human health, animal welfare, and conservation. But the greatest threat is to human rights.

Animal rights leaders frequently equate animal use with Nazism. Carol L. Burnett, PeTA's director of communications, has called biomedical research laboratories "concentration camps for animals."[1] Chris DeRose of Last Chance for Animals says animal studies "are no better than what the Nazis . . . did."[2] A 1986 PeTA press release said, "In time we'll look on those who work in [animal labs] with the horror now reserved for the men and women who experimented on Jews in Auschwitz."[3]

Similarly, when the Buck Center for Research on Aging was established in Marin County, California, in the late 1980s, Elliot Katz of In Defense of Animals described the research lab as "an Auschwitz-like setting."[4] In response, Mary McEachron, director of the center, expressed the shock that all decent people share, when she said, "I find it incredible that someone would compare studies to extend the healthy, productive years of human life to the Holocaust."[5]

Ironically, the Third Reich is the closest the world has ever come to seeing an animal rights regime in practice. A Nazi propaganda magazine made the link between vegetarianism and antivivisection when it posed the questions:

Do you know that your Führer is a vegetarian, and that he does not eat meat because of his general attitude toward life and his love for

123

the world of animals? . . . Do you know that your Führer is an ardent opponent of any torture of animals, in particular of vivisection, which means the scientifically disguised torture of animals, that disgusting product of the Jewish materialistic school in medicine. . . ? [Hitler will] fulfill his role as the savior of animals from continuous and nameless torments and pain . . . by making vivisection illegal.[6]

"By 1936 Hitler was an extremely cranky vegetarian," writes David Irving in *The Secret Diaries of Hitler's Doctor*.[7] John Toland concurs in his biography, *Adolf Hitler*: "After the death of his niece, Geli Raubal, Hitler refused to eat a piece of ham. 'It is like eating a corpse!' he told Göring."[8] Similarly, Henry Spira of Animal Rights International says, "My dream is that people will come to view eating an animal as cannibalism."[9] (Note that the same idea underlay PeTA's 1991 ad equating livestock workers with serial murderer and cannibal Jeffrey Dahmer [chapter 5]).

According to Toland, Hitler's vegetarianism caused him to suffer from chronic flatulence. In *The Mind of Adolf Hitler*, Walter Langer adds that he also suffered from depression, mood swings, irritability, and agitation,[10] all of which are symptoms of vitamin B_{12} deficiency, according to John Lindenbaum in the *New England Journal of Medicine*.[11] Animal products are the only dietary source of vitamin B_{12}.

In a radio broadcast on August 28, 1933, Hermann Göring, head of the German Humane Society and Environmental Minister for the Third Reich, announced:

An absolute and permanent ban on vivisection is not only a necessary law to protect animals and to show sympathy with their pain, but it is also a law for humanity itself. . . . I have therefore announced the immediate prohibition of vivisection and have made the practice a punishable offense in Prussia. Until such time as punishment is pronounced the culprit shall be lodged in a concentration camp.[12]

Göring also banned commercial trapping, severely restricted hunting, regulated the shoeing of horses and boiling of lobsters and crabs, and in one instance sent a fisherman to a concentration camp for cutting up a bait frog.[13] But accusations of "vivisection" proved most valuable as a pretext for rounding up Jewish doctors and scientists.[14]

Camp prisoners were sometimes used as guinea pigs, and often subjected to genuine torture at the hands of Josef Mengele and his ilk. In their crusade to end "the scientifically disguised torture of animals," the Nazis slowly suffocated or froze hundreds of people to death, in experiments where anesthetic and analgesic relief were forbidden.[15]

All sane people are horrified at the idea of such actions. But many animal rights leaders have been publicly ambivalent. For example, Peter Singer has written, "Torturing a human being is almost always wrong, but it is not absolutely wrong."[16]

The position of HSUS that "there is no rational basis for maintaining a moral distinction between the treatment of humans and other animals"[17] should perhaps be read in light of SS Chief Heinrich Himmler's quote when he was rounding up the first prisoners for the concentration camps: "We Germans, who are the only people in the world who have a decent attitude toward animals, will also assume a decent attitude toward these human animals."[18]

In light of the status of infants and retardates in animal rights theory,[19] it is interesting that the death camps started with retardates. Having equated animals with man, the Nazis proceeded to treat men as animals. By the time they were through, the first nation to ban vivisection had rendered countless innocent men, women, and children into lampshades and soap.

This equation continues today. In *Defending Animals' Rights Is the Right Thing to Do*, B. P. Robert Silverman writes, "The Holocaust revealed horror stories about German merchants who sold lampshades made of human skin. But many times more Americans sell fur coats. And aren't fur coats an ugly reminder of those lampshades?"[20]

By assigning "rights" to animals, which are by nature incapable of moral cognition, the Nazis annihilated the very concept of rights.

Ingrid Newkirk wrote a foreword glowing with praise for Silverman's book. Earlier she made the same equation: "Six million people died in concentration camps, but six billion broiler chickens will die this year in slaughterhouses."[21]

No Nazi could have said it better: the Holocaust was no worse than making chicken soup. The victims of Naziism got no worse than they gave to the chickens—they got their just desserts.

This exact rationale was used by the Nazis to shore up antisemitism. Arnold Arluke and Boria Sax wrote, "Antisemitic rhetoric in Germany suggested that persecution of Jews was sometimes perceived as revenge on behalf of aggrieved animals. Jews were identified as enemies of animals and implicitly [of] Germans."[22]

Much of this is replayed today in animal rights. According to Susan Rosenbluth, editor of *The Jewish Voice and Opinion*, "All too often, animal rights activity becomes simply an outlet for old-fashioned antisemitism. Frequent targets are the fur industry (a trade long associated with the Jewish community) and kosher slaughter."[23]

According to one source:

> . . . there is now a mounting campaign with antisemitic overtones to eliminate kosher laws as violating the First Amendment's separation of church and state. Letters to editors are being printed in newspapers in the major cities with kashruth laws condemning such legislation and also branding kosher slaughtering as inhumane. . . .[24]

The article continues: "Helen E. Hones of the Humane Society [HSUS] sued the Secretary of Agriculture . . . for not prosecuting kosher slaughterers as violators of federal law. . . ."[25] Green parties in Sweden and Switzerland have already succeeded in banning kosher slaughter.

In 1992, the American Society for the Prevention of Cruelty to Animals (ASPCA) raided a synagogue in Seagate, Brooklyn, where an ancient ritual of the Jewish High Holy Days was being performed. As prayers are recited, a live chicken is raised over one's head and the sins of the supplicant are transferred to the bird. The ASPCA seized the birds, even though they are not harmed during the ceremony, which dates back to biblical times.

According to the *Jewish Voice and Opinion*, "When the Fur Center

Synagogue on 29th Street in Manhattan was desecrated, the graffiti read: 'What Hitler was to the Jews, furriers are to animals.' "[26] The magazine reprinted a fur advertisement on which a vandal had written: "Hey, Jew-Face, why don't you donate these furs to the homeless, so that the innocent animals will not have died in vain," and "The map of Israel is all over your face and gestures."[27]

When philosopher Carl Cohen of the University of Michigan Medical School wrote an article published in *The New England Journal of Medicine* defending the use of animals in biomedical research, the journal received a number of antisemitic letters, including one reading: "I wish to protest that this unpleasant, objectionable Jew says that animals have no rights. He thinks they may be experimented on and seems to have forgotten the fuss his race made over medical experiments in Germany."[28]

For several years, the group Friends of Animals (FoA) has targeted Leon Hirsch, CEO of United States Surgical Corporation, because his company uses dogs (painlessly) to train surgeons in the use of surgical staples, a replacement for sutures. During this campaign of intimidation and harassment, Hirsch has received a number of anonymous, threatening letters from animal rights activists. Some samples:

You money loving Jew bastard. Your days are numbered. You will die a slow death.

Hello, Leon, are you still killing all those nice dogs. I have your name down to volunteer for a test run in a 12-person microwave oven. Too bad Adolf didn't have microwave ovens in the 40s.

How dare you filthy jews steal innocent animals to torture and slaughter to look for means to make more filthy money. You infiltrate the whole world with venom. It's a shame Hitler did not exterminate each one of you. You're not even human.[29]

FoA protests at U.S. Surgical have featured caricatures of Hirsch as a horned devil, revivals of the "blood libel," and chants of "Kill Hirsch!"[30] On November 11, 1988, an activist named Fran Stephanie

Trutt was arrested in the act of planting two remote-controlled pipe bombs in Hirsch's parking space.[31] When she was convicted, her legal fees were paid by several prominent animal rights groups, including PeTA.[32]

"I reject the idea that humans are superior to other life forms," says Paul Watson, director of the Sea Shepherd Conservation Society, and a founder of Greenpeace. "Man is just an ape with an overly developed sense of superiority."[33] This expresses succinctly an important animal rights contention: man is merely an animal—not morally different from a rat or a cockroach.

On this same premise, the Nazis created eugenic stud farms and brothels for breeding "aryan" stock. They enslaved others as beasts of burden. They used them as involuntary research subjects or as disposable slave workers. They killed the surplus.

In a modern parallel, Sydney Singer, director of an animal rights group called the Good Shepherd Foundation, has established a new religion—the All Beings Are Created Equal (ABACE) Church. He writes, "Human reproduction is like evil perpetuating evil, sickness breeding sickness."[34] He believes his followers ("Abaceites") are more highly evolved than the rest of us. Unlike Abaceites, he writes, our children

> will be participants in cruel, exploitative human societies for many years to come. . . . [M]any creatures shall die as a result of their living. We therefore approve the abortion of babies who are to be reared by alienated human beings. . . . [W]ith the procreation of Abaceites, and the abortion of fetuses of alienated, cruel humans, we hope to achieve our vision. . . ."[35]

Inevitably, human-animal egalitarianism yields to a more thoroughgoing denigration of man and the idealization of animals. British philosopher Patrick Corbett says that "animals are in many respects superior to ourselves."[36] Italian Green Party deputy Fulco Pratesi concludes that "we should be following the animals' example. They are loyal, unwasteful, rational and above all considerate to their own—something humans are not."

As a result of such thinking in Nazi Germany, write Arluke and Sax, "The compassion normally reserved for humans was to be redirected toward animals, and the cold aggressiveness of animal instinct became the model German."[37] Empathy for animals has given way to misanthropy. Jim Mason, coauthor (with Peter Singer) of the vegetarian manifesto *Animal Factories*, writes, "We who have an affinity with nonhuman animals and nature . . . are finding it increasingly difficult to love our fellow 'man.' " Sydney Singer writes, "Humans are exploiters and destroyers, self-appointed world autocrats around whom the universe seems to evolve. . . . As a medical student, I can't afford such misanthropic feelings, but fighting them is a full-time battle."[38] Singer has published a new book, *A Declaration of War: Killing People to Save Animals and the Environment*, in which the author, identified only as "Screaming Wolf," urges activists to "hunt hunters, trap trappers, butcher butchers," and so on.[39]

Reason—an attribute of man that distinguishes him from an animal—is another focus of denigration and attack.

"National Socialism represents the most extreme manifestation of the 20th century revolt against reason," wrote historian Koppel Pinson in *Modern Germany*. "Its basic psychological character was anti-intellectualism."[40]

Philosophers like Martin Heidegger saw reason as "alienating" man from nature. Identifying with animals by suppressing reason and giving rein to the emotions was, for them, a way of "reintegrating" man into nature. Despite the tragic consequences, today many animal rightist intellectuals have espoused this same idea.

A similar disdain of reason and embrace of irrationalism is evident in animal rights today. The real enemy is not capitalism, technology, science, or even *Homo sapiens*, but their common denominator—reason.

Peter Singer kicked off the whole animal rights movement with this thought of Jeremy Bentham: "The question is not, Can they [animals] *reason*, nor Can they *talk*? but Can they *suffer*?"[41]

And who wants reason, or the mind, anyhow? "The human mind is a weak organ, and leads humans astray when it is too greatly relied upon for guidance," writes Syd Singer in *The Earth Religion*. "Humans are basically defective creatures. . . . their minds are their downfall."[42]

Hitler put it best: "We are now at the end of the Age of Reason."[43]

With reason gone, what good are rights? Feminist animal rights writer Marti Kheel believes that "the further divorced human beings are from this instinct or sensibility that nonhuman animals have, the more we seem to require rationality to act as its substitute."[44] She adds, "It is only when our instincts have failed us that we turn to such concepts as rights."[45]

Kheel continues, rather obscurely, "The concept of ethics as a hierarchical set of rules to be superimposed upon the individual does not address the needs of those people (perhaps, mostly women) who feel that their morality or inclinations toward nature reside within themselves."[46] Translating this moral chaos into law, another animal-rights feminist writer, Catharine MacKinnon, urges that we "change one dimension of liberalism as it is embodied in law: the definition of justice as neutrality between abstract categories."[47] As Josephine Donovan, yet another feminist writer in the animal rights camp, explains, "MacKinnon therefore rejects, to use her example, the idea that 'strengthening the free speech of the Klan strengthens the free speech of Blacks.' "[48]

But once MacKinnon establishes that we may censor the Klan, what happens when a majority wants to censor, say, Malcolm X? Ought we to live under some sort of dictatorship to ensure that the rights of bad people are restricted and only politically correct speech is protected? This is precisely how all rights were abolished in Germany.

How is it that the philosophy of animal rights, supposedly an attempt to perfect ethics, has come to motivate such violations of rights?

Peter Singer, the "father of animal rights," does not really believe in rights, human or animal. A true utilitarian, he writes, "there could conceivably be circumstances in which an experiment on an animal stands to reduce suffering so much that it would be permissible to carry it out even if it involved harm to the animal . . . [even if] the animal were a human being."[49]

What if such an experiment required the use of a healthy adult, and could not be performed with anesthetic or analgesic? If no one volunteered, would it be "permissible" to use someone involuntarily? Whom? And who would decide?

Expanding upon animal rights philosopher James Rachels' argument that "eating meat secured through animal farming during a food scarcity is immoral because it is wasteful,"[50] another animal rightist, Clifton Perry, concludes:

> . . . then it should prove doubly unhappy not to exploit a source of meat protein which does not entail waste, i.e., it is not the product of animal farming. . . . Agreement would be expected until it was disclosed that this fantastic source of meat protein consisted of human carrion.[51]

Perry goes on seriously to advocate cannibalizing people who have died of natural causes.

Logically Peter Singer's argument for euthanasia of severely retarded infants would extend to include victims of his "active means of bringing about death" in our menu.

But if our victims may be used for food, why not for lampshades?

"How then, are we to settle these matters?" asks philosopher Tom Regan (author of *The Case for Animal Rights*). "I wish I knew. I am not even certain that they can be settled in a rationally coherent way. . . ."[52]

But rationality is not mandatory to animal rights theory. For Regan goes on to say, "The rights view, I believe, is rationally the most satisfactory moral theory. Of course, if it were possible to show that only human beings were included in its scope, then a person like myself, who believes in animal rights, would be obliged to look elsewhere."[53]

Thus Regan did not ground his philosophy on the general concept of rights and then move logically to include the concept of "animal rights." Rather, he has plucked "animal rights" out of the air as a free-floating abstraction (or faith) and used the broader concept of rights in an attempt to ground his faith.

But were the attempt to fail, and logic prove that only humans could have rights, Regan admits no obligation to abandon animal rights as irrational; rather, he will be "obliged" to abandon rights, and with them, rationality.

At that point, only violence remains. Having lost every scientific and ethical argument, the animal rightists turn to hate, arson, and bombs. Using sophistry, they rationalize that we went to war to stop Naziism and slavery, and animal use "is no better than what the Nazis or slave traders did."[54]

Those who use lies, harassment, intimidation, assault, death threats, and bombs to further their political objectives imitate the tactics of the Brownshirts. Intellectuals who rationalize violence by disparaging reason have adopted the ideological premises of Naziism. And well-meaning but misled donors who finance this movement must bear some of the guilt.

EPILOGUE:

FIGHTING BACK
What You Can Do for People and Animals

In 1990, when I realized that the animal rights movement threatened our important values, I formed Putting People First. Recognizing that few people understood how powerful the animal rights movement had become and how much damage it had already caused, I came to the unhappy conclusion that we were heading for catastrophe.

After several years of active involvement with animal welfare and intense study of the animal rights philosophy, I believe that the animal rights movement is vulnerable. It can be beaten and it must be beaten. The stakes for both people and animals are too high for us to ignore the danger.

Stopping animal rightists will not be easy. They have money, organization, media savvy, and influence in high places. Defeating them will require that everybody who cares about human rights, animal welfare, conservation, and Western culture and values work together.

Putting People First has already caused the animal rights movement some major setbacks. Since we started exposing them in 1990, contributions to major animal rights groups have dropped 10–25 percent.

Animal rights groups are attacking on every front. People who care about human rights, animal welfare, and conservation must become equally determined but, unlike them, we must never lie or break the law.

The media have been made to look like fools by animal rights hoaxes too many times. Thanks to thousands of "letters to the editor" challenging animal extremism, the media are beginning to look at their charges skeptically. Such letters succeeded in exposing Chris DeRose, head of Last Chance for Animals, as a criminal, which resulted in his being fired as animal correspondent for the TV show "Hard Copy." He later went to jail.

Positive stories about animal welfare and critical exposés of animal rights have started appearing in such major publications as the *Washington Post, Christian Science Monitor, Field and Stream, Fortune, People, USA Today,* and the *Economist*; as well as on such television programs as "60 Minutes," "Crossfire," "McLaughlin," "A Closer Look," and "Technopolitics." Rush Limbaugh, the most popular radio talk show host in America, openly ridicules the animal rights agenda.

Industry, conservation, animal welfare, civic, school, and church groups all over North America are becoming active. The Hunters for the Hungry program has served not only to help manage deer herds and feed the poor, but also to educate the public about the role of hunters and game in society.

Over the years, grassroots lobbying has defeated or significantly altered proposed animal rights legislation in many states, including mandatory pet sterilization bills, anti-animal testing bills, and pound seizure bills. A broad citizens' coalition helped defeat a referendum to ban horse-drawn carriages in Washington, D.C., and helped save New York City's carriage horses.

By January 1993, active citizen volunteers had helped enact legislation prohibiting hunter harassment in forty-four states. In 1992, numerous groups allied to defeat Proposition 200, an anti-hunting referendum that would have destroyed wildlife management in Arizona.

On the national level, citizens banded together to oppose a bill introduced by Rep. Charlie Rose of North Carolina that would have legalized animal rights break-ins and even made the victim pay the perpetrator for the cost of the break-in if the burglar "found" (read planted) evidence of violations of Animal Welfare Act regulations.

On the other hand, grassroots activism helped pass the Animal Enterprise Protection Act of 1992 over strenuous animal rights opposition. On one important day, when it appeared that the bill was about to go down a "black hole" in the House Judiciary Committee, Speaker Tom Foley's office was saturated with telephone calls. He ended up walking down the hall to the sponsor of the legislation, Texas Congressman Charlie Stenholm, and saying, "Call off the dogs—you can have your bill!" (Foley couldn't call Stenholm—his phones were all busy!) The law makes burglary, vandalism, arson, bombing, or theft at laboratories, farms, and food facilities a federal offense. The law also requires convicted persons to pay the cost of replacing property, data, records, equipment, or animals destroyed in the attack, as well as reasonable costs of repeating any experimentation that may have been interrupted or invalidated by their attack.

Grassroots volunteers can defeat paid lobbyists.

Animal welfare groups have also been aggressive on the litigation front. In 1993, we filed suit against the U.S. Department of the Interior for violations of the Endangered Species Act. The government, we charged, had been placing species that are not endangered on the endangered species list in flagrant violation of the procedural safeguards written into the act itself—apparently in collusion with animal rights groups.

Farm, conservation, and medical associations are finally working together preparing a full curriculum from kindergarten through Grade 12 on biology, ecology, animal welfare, biomedical research, testing and training animals, wildlife management, conservation, and animal science and agriculture. Meanwhile, volunteers are going into the schools with animals, lecturing on their particular specialty, taking classes on tours of farms or wildlife management areas, and donating books and other materials to their local schools and libraries.

Companies that unthinkingly support animal rights groups for public relations purposes are now regularly inundated with letters from customers asking them to take a closer look at what they are promoting. And when animal rightists arbitrarily pick out a target for boycott and fund-raising attacks, active citizens make sure the victims know they are not alone and we support them.

In one example, animal rights groups launched a boycott against Norwegian companies because (after extensive scientific study) Norway decided to resume sustainable use of the abundant minke whale. Citizen volunteers responded with letters to those companies, urging them to stand up for scientific management. They also started a campaign to "buy out" stocks of their products from store shelves, overwhelming the boycott action.

Successful demonstrations in support of the targets of unfair animal rights attacks are cropping up all over the country. When in 1992 PeTA attacked Wright State University (WSU) researchers in retaliation for their defeat of a pound seizure bill, local volunteers staged a massive demonstration in support of WSU. As a result, for the first time ever, a major media blitz by PeTA turned into widespread criticism of the group.

The list of victories goes on and on, but the point is made, the old saw is true: if you expose animal extremists to daylight, they dry up just like worms.

We have proven that we can take on animal rights extremists and win. Even when we do not win, we force them to devote their resources to controlling their own damage rather than damaging others.

We are encouraged by our successes, but there is much more to be done. The following is what you can do:

Knowledge

1. Be informed about animal rights issues. Read about animal rights. The attached bibliography contains sources you can consult. A subscription to an animal welfare group's newsletter will keep you up to date on the war with animal rights and instruct you on what you can do to participate in the action.

2. When reading newspapers and watching newscasts, pay attention to stories on animal rights and read between the lines. Some stories will openly discuss an animal rights issue, such as burning down a medical research facility or harassing women wearing fur

coats. Others may not be so candid—a tirade against milk, meat, and chickens might be an animal rights gimmick cloaked as a health story.

If you are knowledgeable about animal rights, you will want to get involved.

Participation

3. Get involved with an organization that is fighting animal rights. I've listed a number of good ones in appendix 1. Which you join may depend on your special interests. But if your group focuses on one particular area, such as animal agriculture or zoos, it might be limited. If you want to help form an alliance of all people opposed to the totalitarianism of animal rights, you can join Putting People First.

4. Find out what your organization is doing and volunteer your time. If you become a Friend of the Aquarium, for example, you can hand out information about the good things that aquariums and zoos do to protect endangered species. If someone close to you benefits from medical research in which animals are used in experiments, work with the research center to counter demonstrations by animal rightists who want to shut down its research.

Almost every organization combatting animal rights is poor. Each one needs volunteers to lick and stick envelopes, make phone calls, research and write, provide special services, whatever. If you can contribute stationery or speak at a school or provide legal services, you are needed.

5. Invite representatives from organizations that have been targeted by animal rightists to speak about animal rights issues to groups of which you are a member—a church, business, trade union, civic club, professional association. Other members of your organization may become as interested as you in animal rights.

The Media

6. Write letters to newspapers and magazines about a current issue of animal rights. Perhaps the newspaper has not covered a

story because it does not know the extent of animal rights involvement. Maybe the story is biased in favor of animal rights. Present your arguments in an informed and reasoned way for the greatest impact.

When writing letters keep them short and do not be abusive. Make sure your facts are correct.

7. Adopt a journalist. As you read the newspapers, listen to the news on radio, or watch a local television newscast, determine which newsperson would have the most to gain from learning more about the dangers of animal rights on a particular subject, or who would be more likely to air our point of view. Contact your local journalists and ask them to do stories on the wrongs of animal rights. Encourage the radio shows to invite guests from both sides of the issue to be on call.

8. Get copies of Public Service Announcements and encourage your local radio stations to carry them.

9. Get a copy of "Survival in the High North" and urge your local cable channel to run it.

10. Call in to radio talk shows when they are promoting animal rights and express your view politely. If they are promoting animal welfare, call in and voice your support.

Government

11. Determine how your elected public officials feel about animal rights. Study their records to evaluate their political behavior, or contact us for our questionnaire for legislators or for our PAC candidate rating list. When Election Day comes around—VOTE.

12. Write letters and make telephone calls to the public officials expressing your point of view. If someone is particularly knowledgeable about animal rights and believes in animal welfare, get involved in that official's political campaign at election time; they need lickers and stickers too.

13. Or run yourself. The "other side" is successfully filling elected and nonelected positions. If we care about everything from animal agriculture to medical research and Western culture, we must elect representatives who will enact laws that safeguard them.

And we need to work at every level— not just federal but especially state and local, where many of the most important fights will be waged.

14. When an initiative is placed on your ballot for some trouble-making purpose—banning circuses or rodeos, outlawing the sale of furs, ending horse-drawn carriage rides—volunteer your support to the victims of harassment. Let Putting People First know so we can get involved. We are part of a huge grassroots network that includes wise use, private property, and animal welfare proponents that are always willing to help.

15. Register voters, especially those in your industry, such as farmers, and so on. If they cannot vote, they cannot help us defeat the animal rights movement. Volunteer to help drive voters to and from the polls, or to monitor the voting so the ballot boxes cannot be packed.

Schools

16. If a representative from an animal rights organization comes to a school where you are a student, speak up. Make certain that the representative answers questions about the entire animal rights agenda, such as damaging medical research, closing down circuses and pet shops, preventing restaurants from serving food derived from animal agriculture, and many other matters that often are not mentioned by animal rights advocates. Let your fellow students know about the entire animal rights agenda.

17. If an animal rights representative is invited to speak at your school, ask the school to invite a speaker opposed to animal rights. Suggest a debate. If that is not possible, ask that someone from a counterbalancing organization be given equal time as soon as possible to address the same group of students.

If your school refuses, raise the issue of fairness. Contact a professional association or the Parent Teachers Association for help. If you are an adult, run for the school board. And if necessary, organize a protest rally to highlight the problem.

18. Do what you can to arrange for school trips to farms, medical research laboratories, zoos, and wildlife management centers. Have

the people who work in these places describe how animal rights affects their work.

19. Find out if animal rights propaganda or activities are in your classroom, curriculum, or library. If so, ask school authorities to furnish publications with different points of view.

20. Support science education by championing science teachers who use animals as part of the educational requirements for science courses.

21. Support the freedom of choice for students in school cafeterias. If your school imposes a "Meatless Day," appeal to your educational authorities. Tell them that you approve of vegetarians having a choice of food, but that you should have the same privilege. Point out that a vegetarian diet is unhealthy, lacking B_{12} and other important vitamins that can only be had through meat products.

Hunting

22. If you are a hunter, be sure that you obey the proper hunting rules. Know about the care and use of bows and firearms. Respect posting signs. Do not be a slob hunter. Turn in poachers. Support hunter education programs.

23. Volunteer to take a kid hunting or fishing—and an adult.

24. Support Hunters for the Hungry, which donates extra game meat to homeless shelters. If you are not a hunter, your financial or in-kind contribution can help defray the expenses of meat processing and transportation. Volunteer to work in the food kitchen distributing the venison. And publicize what you are doing so the community learns of your good deeds. Animal rightists do nothing unless they can use it to get publicity—even their terrorist attacks on farms and research labs always come neatly packaged with a press release. We need to learn from them.

Pets

25. If you are a pet lover, take an animal into your home. You can either adopt an animal from the pound or purchase an animal from a breeder, a pet store, or another pet lover.

26. Join your local humane society. If it is being taken over by animal rights zealots, attend hearings and meetings. Take it back. Alert your local newspaper to any illegal or inappropriate use of the organization or its funds for animal rights purposes.

Entertainment

27. When the circus or rodeo is in town, buy a ticket. Take some young people so they will have a chance to see real animals in place of extremist propaganda films.

28. Join an association supporting your local zoo and aquarium.

29. If you belong to an organization, suggest that it rent convention rooms and halls for meetings and social occasions at zoos and aquariums. You will not only enjoy a new kind of setting, but the rental money will be used to benefit animals.

Business

30. Support businesses that have been illegally attacked or unfairly boycotted by animal rights activists. Write the companies to tell them that you are on their side. And buy their products.

31. When you see a television program with a biased animal rights message, write your objections to the sponsor.

32. If a company succumbs to animal rights pressure (for example, stops selling furs or eliminates safety testing), write a letter of complaint to the CEO. Then try to find a different place for your business. If a company stands up to them, show your support by giving them your business. Let your friends and neighbors know in both cases.

Library

33. Make certain that your library contains books that express every viewpoint on animal issues, not just the animal rights' view. If they do not, suggest to the librarians that the other side should have equal billing.

34. Donate books, including this one. Ask that the books you

donate be made part of the reference section to discourage theft. Donate a subscription to an animal welfare group's newsletter.

Furs

35. Wear fur products proudly. Do not let anyone intimidate you.

36. Be sure to tell antifur demonstrators what you think of them, but do it politely, rationally, without profanity. If they are wearing leather, tell them that they like their skins bald, you prefer yours with hair.

Behavior

37. Do not abuse, attack, or harass your animal rights critics. Reason with them, if they seem reasonable, especially in front of an audience. Do not let them drag you into a screaming match. Let them be the only ones out of control.

Your arguments about animal rights are in the mainstream of popular thought. Logic, reason, and common sense are your weapons. When people understand what animal rights is all about, they are horrified and more receptive to our message.

38. Act in lawful ways. *Never, ever resort to illegal actions or justify them when they occur.* Do not copy the violent or unethical tactics of your animal rights adversaries. If laws are passed that adopt an animal rights position, use peaceful and open means to change them. But do not be quiet. Do not accept it lying down. Do something about it.

Police

39. Support police and other law enforcement authorities who are investigating terrorist acts. If you have any information about animal rights vandalism and terrorism that will assist them, come forward with the information.

Children

40. Talk to your children about what they are being taught in their schools. Educate them on the wrongs of animal rights.

41. Be active on your local school board. Join the PTA. Work with the Scouts, YMCA, Future Farmers of America, 4-H, and other groups that deal with children. Be among those who educate them about animal issues. Remember, children like reason and logic; animal welfare is reasonable and logical; animal rights is unreasonable, illogical.

Other

42. Take a friendly pet on a weekly visit to a local nursing home (get your friends to join you). Share your pet for fifteen minutes or an hour with someone who needs a warm, accepting creature to cuddle.

43. If you contribute to the Combined Federal Campaign, list an animal welfare organization to receive your donation.

44. If you think you have been lied to about an industry or activity—the Draize test, so-called factory farming, leg-hold traps, or any other animal use—contact an association representing that use and ask it for an explanation.

No single person or group could possibly think of all the ways to fight animal rights. If you come up with any new ways, please share them with Putting People First. We will pass your ideas along to our forty thousand members and supporters.

The price of freedom is eternal vigilance. The war against our culture and values will continue. We must be proud of what we do and how we live. We must stand up for what we believe. If we continue to ignore the animal rights movement hoping it will go away, we will discover too late that we are too weak to fight back.

If we do nothing, we are certain to lose.

So far, every time an animal welfare group has taken on the

animal rights activists face to face, we have whipped them. If enough of you join in this struggle, we will be able to take them on everywhere.

We can win—we know how. But it will not be easy and no one can do it alone. Someone once said, "All that is necessary for evil to triumph is for good men to do nothing." Let's do something!

APPENDIX 1:

ANIMAL WELFARE ORGANIZATIONS THAT ARE FIGHTING ANIMAL EXTREMISM

Abundant Wildlife Society of
   North America
12665 Highway 59N
Gillette,Wyoming 82716
307–683–2826

Accuracy In Media
1275 K Street, N.W.
Washington, D.C. 20005
202–371–6710

Alliance for America
Box 450
Caroga Lake, New York 12032
518–835–6702

American Agricultural Women
11841 North Mt. Vernon Road
Shannon, Illinois 61078
815–864–2561

American Animal Welfare
   Foundation
405 Sibley Street
St. Paul, Minnesota 55101
612–293–0349

American Association of
   Zoological Parks & Aquariums
797-D Old Georgetown Road
Bethesda, Maryland 20814
301–907–7777

American Farm Bureau
225 Touhy Avenue
Park Ridge, Illinois 60068
312–399–5774

American Fur Industry
101 West 30th Street
New York, New York 10001
212–564–5133

American Horse Council
1700 K Street, N.W. Suite 300
Washington, D.C. 20006
202–296–4031

American Hunting Rights Action
   Committee
919 Prince Street
Alexandria, Virginia 22314
703–684–0550

American Kennel Club
51 Madison Avenue
New York, New York 10010
212–696–8200

American Medical Association
515 North State Street
Chicago, IL 60610
312–464–5382

American National Cattle Women
PO Box 3881
Englewood, Colorado 80155
303–694–0313

American Sheep Industries
   Association
6911 South Yosemite Street
Englewood, Colorado 80112
303–771–3500

American Veal Association
10009 Kensington Parkway
Kensington, Maryland 20895
301–942–6121

Americans for Medical Progress
Crystal Square Three
17035 Jefferson Davis Highway
Suite 907
Arlington, Virginia 22202
703–486–1411

Animal Industry Foundation
1501 Wilson Boulevard
Suite 1100
Arlington, Virginia 22209
703–524–0810

Archery Manufacturer's
   Organization
2622 C-4, N.W. 43rd Street
Gainesville, Florida 32606
904–377–8262

A Wisconsin Alliance for
   Resources in the Environment,
   Inc.
PO Box 352
Fort Atkinson, Wisconsin 53538
414–563–6209

Barn Tours
PO Box 442
Templeton, California 93465
805–239–9150

Canadian Trappers Alliance
Williamsburg, York County
New Brunswick E0H-1T0 Canada
506–367–2652

Carriage Operators of North
   America
17790 Cooper Road
Nevada City, California 95959
916–265–5348

Circus Fans of America
6 Stratton Court
Potomac, Maryland 20854
301–762–8272

Coalition for Animals & Animal
   Research
PO Box 8060
Berkeley, California 94707–8060
510–642–0308
   and
PO Box 22441
San Diego, California 92192

Congressional Sportsmen's Caucus
729 15th Street, N.W.
Suite 700
Washington, D.C. 20005
202–628–8724

Cosmetics, Toiletries, & Fragrances
  Association
1101 17th Street, N.W.
Suite 300
Washington, D.C. 20036
202–331–1770

Council of Athabascan Tribal
  Governments
PO Box 33
Fort Yukon, Alaska 99740
907–662–2587

Federation Des Chasseurs L'Arc
33 rue de La Haie Coq
93308 Aubervilliers Cedex,
  France
011–33–1–43–52–3708

The Fishermen's Coalition
826 Orange Avenue
Suite 504
Coronado, California 92118
619–575–4664

Foundation for Biomedical
  Research
818 Connecticut Avenue, N.W.
Suite 303
Washington, D.C. 20006
202–457–0654

Foundation Internationale
  Pour la Sauvegarde de
  Gibier
15 Rue de Teheran
Paris, France
011–33–1–45–63–5133

Friends of Rodeo
625 Eighteenth Street
Plano, Texas 75074
214–424–4554

Fur Bearers Unlimited
P.O. Box 4129
Bloomington, Illinois 61702
309–829–7615

Fur Counsil of Canada
1435 Rue St.-Alexandre
Suite 1270
Montreal, Quebec
H3A-264 Canada
800–361–1626

Fur Farm Animal Welfare
  Coalition
225 East 6th Street
Suite 230
St. Paul, Minnesota 55101
612–293–0349

Fur Information Council of
  America
447A Carlisle Drive
Herndon, Virginia 22070
703–471–5238

Game Conservation International
PO Box 17444
San Antonio, Texas 78217
210–824–7509

Gwichin Steering Committee
PO Box 202768
Anchorage, Alaska 99520
907–258–6814

Heifer Project International
Route 2, Box 33
Perryville, Arkansas 72126
501–889–5124

High North Alliance
Box 123, N 8390 Reine
Lofoten Islands, Norway
47–88–92–414

The Hunters' Alliance
205 Main Street
Drawer B
Stevensville, Montana 59870
406–777–2521

incurably ill for Animal Research
PO Box 27454
Lansing, Michigan 48909
517–887–1141

Livestock Marketing Association
7509 Tiffany Springs Parkway
Kansas City, Missouri 64153
816–891–0502

Mid States Rodeo Association
6920 Bear Swamp Road
Medina, Ohio 44256
216–336–7080

Mountain States Legal Foundation
1660 Lincoln Street
Suite 2300
Denver, Colorado 80264
303–861–0244

National American Gamebird
    Association
PO Box 96
Goose Lake, Iowa 52750
319–242–3046

National Animal Interest Alliance
PO Box 66579
Portland, Oregon 97290
503–761–8962

National Association for
    Biomedical Research
818 Connecticut Avenue, N.W.
Suite 303
Washington, D.C. 20006
202–857–0540

National Bowhunters Education
    Foundation
PO Box 543
Rockton, Illinois 61072
815–624–4495

National Cattlemen's Association
5420 S. Quebec Street
PO Box 3469
Englewood, Colorado 80255
303–694–0305

National Dairy Association
723 Yost Road
West Alexandria, Ohio 45381
513–456–2054

National Pork Producers
501 School Street, S.W.
Suite 400
Washington, D.C. 20024
202–554–3690

National Rifle Association
1600 Rhode Island Avenue, N.W.
Washington, D.C. 20036
202–828–6000

National Shooting Sports
    Foundation
555 Danbury Road
Wilton, Connecticut 06897
203–762–1320

National Trappers Association
PO Box 3667
Bloomington, Illinois 61701
309–829–2422

National Turkey Federation
11319 Sunset Hills Road
Reston, Virginia 22090
703–435–7208

National Wild Turkey
 Federation
PO Box 530
Edgefield, South Carolina 29824
803-637-3106

National Wool Growers
 Association
425 13th Street, N.W.
Suite 826
Washington, D.C. 20004

New Mexico Wool Growers
805 North Richardson
PO Box 220
Roswell, New Mexico 88202
505-623-1699

North American Rodeo
 Commission
PO Box 1144
Camp Hill, Pennsylvania 17011
717-783-3256

Pacific Egg & Poultry
 Association
1620 North Carpenter Road
Suite A-4
Modesto, California 95351-1145
209-524-9666

Partners in Research
PO Box 192
Station "B"
London, Ontario
N6A-4V6 Canada
519-433-7866

People for the West!
301 N. Main
Pueblo, Colorado 81003
719-543-8421

Pharmaceutical Manufacturers
 Association
1100 15th Street, N.W.
Washington, D.C. 20005
202-835-3460

Project Wild
Salina Star Route
Boulder, Colorado 80302
303-444-2390

Putting People First
4401 Connecticut Avenue, N.W.
Suite 310-A
Washington, D.C. 20008
202-364-7277

Safari Club International
4800 West Gates Pass Road
Tucson, Arizona 85745
602-620-1220

Southwest Meat Association
2401 Avenue J
Suite 211
Arlington, Texas 76006
817-640-7728

State Poultry Industry
 Coordinated Effort
PO Box 821
Ithaca, New York 14850
518-584-5912

Ted Nugent World Bowhunters
4008 W. Michigan Avenue
Jackson, Michigan 49202
517-570-9060

United Bowhunters of New Jersey
5117 Somers Point
Mays Landing, New Jersey 08330
609-625-4486

United Conservation Alliance
PO Box 820706
Houston, Texas 77282–0706
713–558–1399

United Egg Producers
3951 Snapfinger Parkway
Suite 580
Decatur, Georgia 30035
404–288–6700

United Kennel Club
100 E. Kilgore Road
Kalamazoo, Michigan 49001
616–343–9020

Unified Sportsmen of
   Pennsylvania
824 Dorsea Road
Lancaster, Pennsylvania
   17601

Wildlife Legislative Fund of
   America
801 Kingsmill Parkway
Columbus, Ohio 43229
614–888–4868

Wildlife Management Institute
1101 14th Street, N.W.
Suite 725
Washington, D.C. 20005
202–371–1808

Women Involved in Farm
   Economics
Route 1, Box 224
Bradshaw, Nebraska 68319
402–736–4427

World Animal Resource Network
RR #4
Wharton, Ontario
NOH-270 Canada
519–534–4151

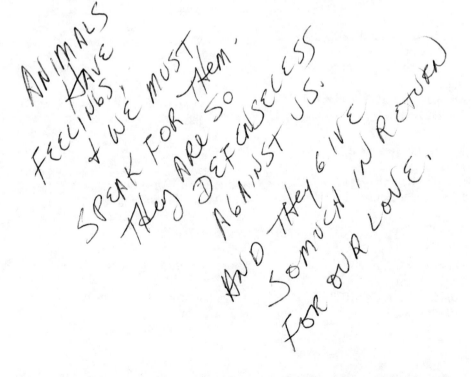

APPENDIX 2:

U.S. ANIMAL RIGHTS GROUPS

PLEASE SUPPORT THESE GROUPS BE KIND TO ANIMALS

(Most active groups are in bold)

Action for Animals
Oakland, CA

Activists for Protective Animal
   Legislation
Costa Mesa, CA

Actors and Others for Animals
North Hollywood, CA

Alaska Wildlife Alliance
Anchorage, AK

All Beings Are Created Equal
   Church
Grass Valley, CA

Alliance for Animals
Boston, MA

Alliance for Animals, Inc.
Madison, WI

Alliance for Research
   Accountability
Ventura, CA

**American Anti-Vivisection
   Society
Philadelphia, PA**

American Defenders Against
   Animal Mistreatment
Wilmington, DE

American Fund for Alternatives to
   Animal Research
New York, NY

American Horse Protection
   Association
New York, NY

American Humane Education
   Society
Boston, MA

**American Society for the
Prevention of Cruelty to
Animals
New York, NY**

American Vegan Society
Malaga, NJ

American Vegetarians
Akron, OH

Animal Advocates, Inc.
Pittsburgh, PA

Animal Aid
Portland, OR

Animal Allies
Los Angeles, CA

Animal Avengers
Unlisted

151

Animal Defense Legion
Santa Rosa, CA

**Animal Legal Defense Fund
San Rafael, CA**

Animal Liberation
New York, NY

**Animal Liberation Front
Unlisted**

Animal Liberation Front Support
Group of America
San Bernadino, CA

Animal Liberation League
Arlington, TX

Animal Peace
New Orleans, LA

Animal Political Action Committee
Washington, DC

**Animal Protection Institute of
America
Sacramento, CA**

Animal Protective Association, Inc.
Leesburg, VA

Animal Rescue League
Boston, MA

Animal Rights Action League
Saratoga Springs, NY

Animal Rights Advocates of
Western New York
Amherst, NY

Animal Rights Alliance
Westport, CT

Animal Rights Coalition
Bloomington, MN

Animal Rights Coalitions
New York, NY

Animal Rights Community
Cincinnati, OH

Animal Rights Connection
San Francisco, CA

Animal Rights Forum
Montpelier, VT

Animal Rights Front
New Haven, CT

Animal Rights Information and
Education Service
Rowayton, CT

**Animal Rights International
New York, NY**

Animal Rights Militia
Unlisted

Animal Rights Mobilization
Williamsport, PA

**Animal Rights Network, Inc.
Monroe, CT**

Animal Rights of Texas
Fort Worth, TX

**Animal Welfare Institute
Washington, DC**

Animals Emancipation
Goleta, CA

Animals Lobby
Sacramento, CA

Anti-Cruelty Society
Chicago, IL

Argus Archives
New York, NY

Arizonans for Safety and Humanity
on Public Lands
Phoenix, AZ

Association of Veterinarians for
  Animal Rights
New York, NY

Band of Mercy
Unlisted

Beauty Without Cruelty
New York, NY

Berkeley Students for Animal
  Liberation
Berkeley, CA

Between the Species
Berkeley, CA

Beyond Beef Coalition
Washington, DC

Bluegrass Animal Welfare League
Lexington, KY

Brighton Students for Peaceful
  Change
Rochester, NY

Buddhists Concerned for Animals,
  Inc.
San Francisco, CA

Californians for the Ethical
  Treatment of Animals
Morongo Valley, CA

Capital Area Humane Society
Columbus, OH

Carriage Horse Action Committee
New York, NY

Center for Environmental
  Education
Washington, DC

Center for Respect of Life and the
  Environment
Washington, DC

Citizens for Animal Rights
Peoria, IL

Citizens for Animals
Clarks Summit, PA

Citizens for Animals, Resources
  and Environment
Milwaukee, WI

Clergy/Friends for Animals/Earth
Summit, NJ

Coalition Against Fur Farms
Ashland, OR

Coalition for Pet Population
  Control
Los Angeles, CA

Coalition to End Animal Suffering
  and Exploitation
Cambridge, MA

Coalition to Protect Animals in
  Entertainment
Riverside, CA

Coalition to Update Research and
  Education
New York, NY

Committee for Animal Rights and
  Education
Oceanville, NJ

Committee for Humane
  Legislation
Washington, DC

Committee to Abolish Sport
  Hunting
White Plains, NY

Compassion for Animals
  Foundation
Culver City, CA

Concerned Citizens for Animals, Inc.
Springfield, MA

Congressional Friends of Animals
Washington, DC

Culture and Animals Foundation
Raleigh, NC

Defenders of Animal Rights, Inc.
Phoenix, MD

Defenders of Wildlife
Washington, DC

Dedication and Everlasting Love to Animals
Glendale, CA

Disabled Against Animal Research and Exploitation
Washington, DC

Doris Day Animal League
Washington, DC

Earth First!
Tucson, AZ

Earth Island Institute
San Francisco, CA

Earthsave Foundation
Felton, CA

Earthtrust
Honolulu, HI

Eco-Dykes
Unlisted

Elsa Wild Animal Appeal
Elmhurst, IL

End Dogs on Earth Now!
Unlisted

Environmental Investigation Agency
Washington, DC

Farm Animal Reform Movement
Washington, DC

Farm Freedom Fighters
Unlisted

Farm Sanctuary
Rockland, DE

Feminists for Animal Rights
Berkeley, CA

Florida Action for Animals, Inc.
Stuart, FL

Focus on Animals
Trumbull, CT

Food Animal Concerns Trust, Inc.
Chicago, IL

Friends of Animals and Their Environment
Minneapolis, MN

Friends of Animals, Inc.
Norwalk, CT

Friends of Beaversprite
Little Falls, NY

Fund For Animals, Inc.
New York, NY

Global Investigations
Scotts Valley, CA

Good Shepherd Foundation
Nevada City, CA

Green Animal Liberation Caucus
Kansas City, MO

Greenpeace U.S.A.
Washington, DC

Hawaii Animal Welfare Cooperative
Hilo, HI

Houston Animal Rights Team
Houston, TX

Human/Animal Liberation Front
Unlisted

Humane Education Committee
New York, NY

Humane Education Network
Menlo Park, CA

**Humane Farming Association
San Francisco, CA**

**Humane Society of the United
States
Washington, DC**

Humane Task Force
Winnetka, CA

Humans Against Rabbit
Exploitation
Williamsport, PA

Hunt Saboteurs
Santa Cruz, CA

**In Defense of Animals
San Rafael, CA**

Independent Animal Activists
Network
Sioux Falls, SD

International Animal Rights
Alliance
Boston, MA

International Defenders of Animals
San Martin, CA

**International Fund for Animal
Welfare
Varmouth Port, MA**

International Network for Religion
and Animals
Washington, DC

**International Primate Protection
League
Summerville, SC**

**International Society for Animal
Rights, Inc.
Clarks Summit, PA**

International Wildlife Coalition
Falmouth, MA

Jehovah's Witnesses for Animal
Rights
Sunnyvale, CA

Jews for Animal Rights
Marblehead, MA

Kalamazoo-Area Animal
Liberation League
Kalamazoo, MI

**Last Chance for Animals
Tarzana, CA**

Legislation in Support of Animals
New Orleans, LA

Lehigh Valley Animal Rights
Coalition
Allentown, PA

Lifeline for Wildlife, Inc.
Stony Point, NY

**Lynx Educational Fund for Animal
Welfare, Inc.
Monroe, CT**

Maine Animal Coalition
Old Orchard Beach, ME

Maine Citizens for Trapping
Reform
Searsport, ME

**Massachusetts Society for the
Prevention of Cruelty to
Animals
Boston, MA**

Meat Mission
Unlisted

Medical Research Modernization
Committee
New York, NY

Mercy Crusade, Inc.
Van Nuys, CA

Michigan Humane Society
Detroit, MI

Millennium Guild
New York, NY

Mobilization for Animals
Pittsburgh, PA

National Alliance for Animal
Legislation
Washington, DC

National Alliance for Animals
Washington, DC

National Alliance for Animals
Educational Fund
Washington, DC

National Animal Legal Foundation
Sacramento, CA

National Anti-Vivisection Society
Chicago, IL

National Association for Humane
and Environmental Education
East Haddam, CT

National Association of Nurses
Against Vivisection
Washington, DC

National Coalition to Protect Our
Pets, Inc.
Los Angeles, CA

National Foundation for Animal
Law
Sacramento, CA

National Humane Education
Society
Leesburg, VA

National Society of Musicians for
Animals
Redding Ridge, CT

Naturists Advocating Vegetarian
and Environmental Lifestyles
Austin, TX

Network for Ohio Animal Action
Cleveland, OH

New England Anti-Vivisection
Society
Boston, MA

New Hampshire Animal Rights
League
Northfield, NH

New Jersey Animal Rights Alliance
Woodbridge, NJ

New York State Coalition for
Animals
Albany, NY

New York State Humane
Association, Inc.
New Paltz, NY

Noah's Friends
Richmond, VA

North Carolina Network for
Animals
Greensboro, NC

Northwest Animal Rights Network
Seattle, WA

Ohio Humane Education
Association
Grove City, OH

Orange County People for Animals
Santa Ana, CA

Our Animal Wards
Washington, DC

Paint Panthers
Unlisted

Peaceable Kingdom
Chicago, IL

Peninsula Humane Society
San Mateo, CA

Pennsylvania Animal Welfare
   Society
Philadelphia, PA

Pennsylvania Society for the
   Prevention of Cruelty to
   Animals
Philadelphia, PA

People for Animal Rights
Syracuse, NY

**People for the Ethical Treatment of
   Animals
Washington, DC**

**Performing Animal Welfare
   Society
Galt, CA**

**Physicians Committee for
   Responsible Medicine
Washington, DC**

Political Action Committee for
   Animal Welfare and Protection
Columbus, OH

Political Animal Welfare Action
   Committee
San Ramon, CA

Prairie Dog Rescue, Inc.
Englewood, CO

**Primarily Primates
San Antonio, TX**

**Progressive Animal Welfare
   Society
Seattle, WA**

Project Wolf, USA
Seattle, WA

Protect Our Earth's Treasures
Columbus, OH

Protective Association for World
   Species, Inc.
New Berlin, WI

**Psychologists for the Ethical
   Treatment of Animals
New Gloucester, ME**

**Rocky Mountain Humane Society
Littleston, CO**

San Diego Animal Advocates
Vista, CA

San Francisco Society for the
   Prevention of Cruelty to
   Animals
San Francisco, CA

Sangre de Christo Animal
   Protection
Santa Fe, NM

Sarasota In Defense of Animals
Sarasota, FL

Save Pound Animals from Research
   Experiments
Costa Mesa, CA

Save the Animals Fund, Inc.
Los Angeles, CA

Scientists Group for the Reform of
   Animal Experimentation
Whitestone, NY

Sea Shepherd Conservation Society
Redondo Beach, CA

Society of Activist Vegetarians
Charleston, WV

Society Against Vivisection
Costa Mesa, CA

Society for Animal Protective
Legislation
Washington, DC

Society for Animal Rights
Liano, CA

Sonoma County People for Animal
Rights
Santa Rosa, CA

South Florida Animal Activists
Fort Lauderdale, FL

Spokane People for the Ethical
Treatment of Animals
Spokane, WA

Student Action Corps for Animals,
Inc.
Washington, DC

Students United Protesting
Research Experiments on Sen-
tient Subjects
Pasadena, CA

Tennessee Network for Animals
Knoxville, TN

Texas Humane Information
Network
Austin, TX

True Friends
Unlisted

Unexpected Wildlife Refuge, Inc.
Newfield, NJ

United Action for Animals
New York, NY

United Activists for Animal Rights
Riverside, CA

United Animal Defenders, Inc.
Cleveland, OH

United Animal Nations, USA.
Sacramento, CA

United Humanitarians
Philadelphia, PA

University Students Against
Vivisection
Fullerton, CA

Vegan Network
Orange, CA

Vegetarian Information Service,
Inc.
Pocasset, MA

Virginia Federation of Humane
Societies, Inc.
Woodbridge, VA

Vivisection Investigation League
New York, NY

Voice for Animals
San Antonio, TX

Voice of Nature Network
Westport, CT

Voices for Animals
Charlottsville, VA

Voices for Animals
Tucson, AZ

Voices for Animals of Central
Florida, Inc.
Winter Park, FL

Wasatch Humane
Farmington, UT

Western North Carolina Animal
  Rights Coalition
Asheville, NC

Westside Animal Action Network
Venice, CA

Wild Horse and Burro Sanctuary
Shingletown, CA

Wildlife Refuge Reform Coalition
Washington, DC

Women's Wilderness Warriors
Unlisted

Woodstock Animal Rights
  Movement
Woodstock, NY

World Society for the Protection of
  Animals
Boston, MA

Youngstown Area Animal
  Protectionists, Inc.
Youngstown, OH

Zero Population Growth
Washington, DC

APPENDIX 3:

A DECADE OF ANIMAL EXTREMISM, 1984–1993

(Partial List)

7/16/93 Coalition Against Fur Farms (CAFF) founder Rodney Coronado indicted by federal grand jury for arson at Michigan State University (see 2/28/92).

7/6/93 Fake bombs planted at homes of 5 biomedical researchers in Montgomery County, Maryland (see 3/27/93).

6/24/93 Yale University computer scientist involved in animal research badly injured by mail bomb; immediately thereafter, his brother, another animal researcher, received the phone threat: "You're next."

6/22/93 University of California at San Francisco geneticist maimed by mail bomb.

5/24/93 Animal Liberation Action Foundation (ALAF) sends letter threatening "bloodletting" to 3 biomedical researchers and 2 consumer products manufacturing companies.

5/18/93 Three members of the Vegan Front sentenced to 1 year in jail for vandalizing fur stores in Memphis, Tennessee.

3/27/93 "Animal Avengers" admit responsibility for vandalizing the homes of 5 biomedical researchers in Montgomery County, Maryland.

11/8/92 ALF arson, Swanson Meats, Minneapolis, Minnesota. Five trucks firebombed—$100,000 in damages.

10/28/92 PeTA infiltrator Virginia Lee Bollinger arrested for disorderly conduct, Wright State University, Fairborn, Ohio.

10/24/92 ALF arson, USDA Predator Research Facility, Millville, Utah, and Utah State University at Logan. Seven coyotes injured, 2 killed, 1 missing—$110,000 in damages.

7/20/92 PeTA founders Ingrid Newkirk and Alex Pacheco respond to grand jury subpoena to provide fingerprints and handwriting samples to Federal Bureau of Investigation.

6/24/92 ALF member Darren Todd Thurston arrested for arson in Canada with cache of semiautomatic weapons and practice grenades.

6/1/92 ALF break-in, University of Alberta in Edmonton, Ontario.

2/28/92 ALF arson at Michigan State University. Dr. Richard Aulerich lost 32 years of research on pollution and wildlife diseases. Dr. Karen Chou lost 10 years of work on in vitro-research—$100,000 in damages.

12/15/91 ALF arson, Billingsgate Fish Company, Edmonton, Ontario.

12/91 ALF arson, Malecky Mink Ranch, Yamhill, Oregon.

11/13/91 Ten ALF members arrested in London for conspiracy to contaminate bottles of Lucozade, a soft drink manufactured by SmithKline Beecham Ltd., Britain's second-largest manufacturer of pharmaceuticals, to force the company to stop using animals in biomedical research and testing.

8/12/91 ALF arson, Washington State University at Pullman. Seven coyotes, 6 mink, and 10 mice released. Most of the coyotes later found roadkilled.

6/91 ALF arson, Northwest Farm Food Cooperative, Edmonds, Washington.

6/10/91 ALF arson, Oregon State University.

1/1/91 ALF theft, Hektoen Laboratory, Cook County Hospital, Chicago. Eleven rabbits, 10 guinea pigs, and an undetermined number of rats stolen. Delayed research on treating burns and gastrointestinal research.

12/10/90 PeTA loses $3.1 million defamation judgment to Las Vegas animal trainer Bobby Berosini.

1/13/90 ALF burglary, office of Dr. Adrian Morrison, University of Pennsylvania, for speaking out in defense of animal research.

1/8/90 FoA activist Fran Stephanie Trutt convicted of the attempted murder (11/11/88) of Leon Hirsch, president of U.S. Surgical Company. Her legal fees paid by PeTA.

7/4/89 ALF burglary, Texas Tech University Health Science Center. Dr.

John Orem's research on Sudden Infant Death Syndrome (SIDS) destroyed, 5 cats stolen—$70,000 in damages.

5/28/89   ALF-attempted firebombing, California Cattlemen's Association, Sacramento.

4/28/89   ALF-attemped firebombing, Luce-Carmel Meat Company, Montery, California.

4/24/89   ALF arson, Windsor Meats, Kentucky Fried Chicken, Nazare Market, Hycrest Meat Market, Vancouver, Canada.

4/2/89   ALF arson, University of Arizona at Tucson. Over 1,000 mice infected with cryptosporidium, a potentially fatal contagion, released—$100,000 in damages.

3/26/89   Death threats against a researcher spray painted on buildings at Northwestern University, Evanston, Illinois.

2/26/89   Burglary, Duke University, Durham, North Carolina.

1/29/89   Earth First! arson, Dixon Livestock Company, Sacramento—$250,000 in damages.

9/24/88   Seven people arrested in the act of breaking in, University of California at Santa Cruz.

8/15/88   ALF burglary, Loma Linda University. Seven dogs, research records stolen, vandalism—$10,000 in damages.

6/14/88   Mysterious disappearance of 200 beavers from farm being managed in receivership by PeTA. Beavers were slated to be sold to pay off farm's debts. Stevensville, Montana.

4/21/88   LCA break-in, UCLA Brain Research Institute, Davis, California.

4/4/88   ALF burglary, Davis Poultry and Egg Ranch, 28 hens stolen.

3/27/88   Nitabell Rabbitry, California. Twenty-four rabbits stolen.

3/23/88   ALF member Roger Troen sentenced for burglary, University of Oregon (10/26/86). One hundred and fifty cats, rabbits, rats, and hamsters stolen—$50,000 in damages.

1/29/88   ALF burglary, University of California at Irvine. Thirteen beagles used in lung research stolen.

8/23/87   Band of Mercy burglary, USDA Animal Parasitology Institute, Beltsville, Maryland. Seven pigs, 27 cats infected with potentially dangerous bacteria, stolen.

8/12/87   ALF burglary, University of Nevada, Las Vegas. Three goats stolen.

6/2/87   Firebombing, Hallmark Furs, St. Louis, Missouri—$1 million in damages.

6/13/87   ALF burglary, University of California at Davis. Five turkey vultures stolen.

5/24/87   Western Wildlife Unit burglary, Bureau of Land Management, Litchfield, California. Six horses stolen.

4/18/87   Farm Freedom Fighters burglary, Wolfe Poultry Farms, Milan, Pennsylvania. Forty chickens stolen.

4/16/87   ALF burglary, rabbit breeding farm, San Bernadino County, California. One hundred rabbits stolen.

4/16/87   ALF arson, Animal Diagnostic Clinic, University of California at Davis—$5.1 million in damages.

6/4/86   Farm Freedom Fighters burglary, Sydel's Egg Farm, Hartley, Delaware. Twenty-five chickens stolen.

5/19/86   Vandalism, Simonsen Laboratories, Gilroy, California. Twelve thousand rodents exposed to contaminants, equipment destroyed—$165,000 in damages.

2/27/86   IDA linked to threats against at least 40 university presidents.

9/9/85   HALF demonstrators hurl axe into front door of home of principal investigator, New York State Psychiatric Institute.

4/20/85   ALF burglary, University of California at Riverside. Four hundred and sixty rats, mice, pigeons, monkeys, cats, rabbits, opossums, and gerbils stolen—$600,000 in damages.

6/84   Folsom Rodeo, Sacramento, California, vandalized.

5/31/84   ALF burglary, University of Pennsylvania Head Injury Laboratory. Six years of research data stolen, equipment destroyed.

APPENDIX 4:

USING ANIMALS IN BIOMEDICAL RESEARCH
An Overview

Thousands of years ago, spears and arrows freed our ancestors from deadly predators.

Today, biomedical research is freeing millions of people around the world from equally deadly viruses and parasitic diseases.

Biomedical researchers study many different things, including computers, cell cultures, cadavers, live animals, and human volunteers. Live animals have been the most valuable models of all. The results of animal research include modern anesthetics and analgesics (pain killers). Today they help you at the doctor or dentist's office, and your pet at the veterinarian's office. They also help to make most research today painless for both animals and human volunteers.

FACT: According to the United States Department of Agriculture:
- 93% of animals used in research in the United States experience no pain or have it alleviated.
- 58% are not subjected to painful stimuli.
- 35% are given anesthetics and/or analgesics.
- 7% experience some pain. This includes those in studies to help the 300,000 Americans who fall victim to chronic pain each year.

Biomedical research using animals has produced vaccines and cures for many diseases that harm both people and animals.

Today, animal research holds the key to treating and preventing diseases like childhood leukemia, cancer, and AIDS.

What Has Animal Research Given Us?

THERAPIES AND PROCEDURES:

anesthesia	organ transplantation
chemotherapy	bone marrow transplants
insulin	phototherapy
cardiac catheterization	the artificial heart
intravenous feeding	cortisone
tranquilizers	laproscopic surgery
skin grafting	microsurgery
thyroxin	corneal transplantation
hip replacement surgery	monoclonal antibodies
artificial limbs	xenotransplantation
antibiotics	

VACCINES FOR:

poliomyletis	tuberculosis
rubella	cholera
diphtheria	mumps
whooping cough	chickenpox
smallpox	measles
tetanus	yellow fever

TREATMENTS FOR:

cancer	leprosy
diabetes	hypertension
Hodgkin's disease	ulcers
river blindness	mental illness
jaundice	arthritis
beriberi	asthma
pellagra	epilepsy

FACT: Virtually every medical advance of the twentieth century has resulted from animal research. Research using animals has extended our life expectancy by more than *28 years*!

Animals in Research

Animals	Diseases shared with man	Past results of animal research	Subjects of animal research today
RATS AND MICE			
90 to 95 percent of animals used in research are rats or mice.	anemia arthritis cancer cataracts diabetes hypertension lupus muscular dystrophy	antibiotics cancer chemotherapy intravenous feeding tranquilizers discovery of DNA monoclonal antibodies	Alzheimer's disease cancer muscular dystrophy consumer safety tests bone research kidney disease
DOGS AND CATS			
Dogs and cats put together make up less than 1.5% of animals used in research. For each one used in research, about 50 are killed in animal shelters.	*(dogs)* arthritis breast cancer glaucoma diabetes heart defects hemophilia kidney disease *(cats)* breast cancer diabetes hyperthyroidism leukemia the common cold	antibiotics cardiac catheterization intravenous feeding treatment for pellagra hypertension histamine shock rickets kidney disease artificial heart	*(dogs)* cardiovascular research life-saving techniques glaucoma cataracts *(cats)* brain & neurological research leukemia deafness, tinnitis Sudden Infant Death Syndrome
PRIMATES			
Primates make up about 0.5% of animals used in research. Those used are bred in captivity, not captured from the wild.	atherosclerosis hepatitis diabetes poliomyletis hyaline membrane disease malaria	Rh factor treatment of hepatitis B cerebral revascularization neo-natal care cure for rubella cortisone cancer chemotherapy tranquilizers treatment for pellagra treatment for leprosy corneal transplantation	Alzheimer's disease atheriosclerosis anesthesia research cyclosporin heart disease Parkinson's disease periodontal disease polio vaccine heart disease AIDS

How Other Animals in Research Help You

OPOSSUM

immunology research
reproductive research
genetic research

FERRETS

vision

SNAKES

anti-venom serums
analgesics
diagnostic tests

ARMADILLOS

leprosy & other infectious diseases
reproductive & genetic research

RABBITS

monoclonal antibodies
immunology
treatment for high blood pressure
rheumatoid arthritis
cancer chemotherapy
cardiac catheterization
intravenous feeding
tranquilizers
whooping cough vaccine

Animals Benefit from Animal Research, Too!

ANIMAL RESEARCH HAS PRODUCED TREATMENTS FOR MANY ANIMAL ILLNESSES:

hookworm
heartworm
Giardia
feline dilated cardiomyopathy
tuberculosis

rickets
white muscle disease
brain tumors
birth defects
cancer

HOW SPECIFIC ANIMALS BENEFIT

Cattle	Dogs	Cats
tetanus	rabies	feline leukemia
leptospirosis	distemper	rabies
brucellocis	parvovirus	feline enteritis
	infectious hepatitis	rhinotracheitis
	parainfluenza	pneumonitis
	leptospirosis	

OTHER ANIMALS

Pigs	Sheep	Horses	Poultry

USED TO STUDY:

Pigs	Sheep	Horses	Poultry
antibiotics	obstetric analgesics	diptheria	atherosclerosis
organ transplants	fetal hormones		antibiotics
diabetes	fetal cardiology		treatment for beriberi
heart disease	pregnancy		
osteoporosis			
arthritis			
wound healing			

BENEFIT BY VACCINES OR TREATMENTS FOR:

Pigs	Sheep	Horses	Poultry
influenza	anthrax	strangles	Newcastle disease
swine erysipelas	bluetongue	tetanus	Marek's disease
		encephalomyletis	fowl cholera
		rabies	duck hepatitis
			hemorrhagic enteritis
			fowl typhoid
			fowl pox

FACT: Since 1968, the number of animals used in research in the United States has been reduced by 40 percent.

Twentieth-Century Miracles

THE HISTORY OF ANIMAL RESEARCH AND
BIOMEDICAL BREAKTHROUGHS

Items in Boldface are Nobel Prize-Winners

1901   **Development of diphtheria antiserum**
Understanding of malaria life cycle
Animal responses to various stimuli
Tuberculosis studies
Characterization of central nervous system
Role of protozoa as cause of disease
Immune reactions and functions of phagocytes

1910   **Nuclear protein cell chemistry**
Cardiac catheterization techniques
Understanding of nutrition
Suture, grafting blood vessels
Treatment for rickets
Treatment for histamine shock
Mechanisms of anaphylaxis
Components of blood, plasma
Treatment for pellagra
Mechanisms of immunity
Surgical techniques

1920   **Capillary motor regulating system**
Oxygen and lactic acid muscle metabolism
Discovery of insulin and control of diabetes
Intravenous feeding
Electrocardiography
Ventilation of open thorax
Pathogenesis of typhus
Discovery of thyroxin
Discovery of antineuretic and growth stimulating vitamins

1930   **Functions of neurons**
Development of modern anesthesia
Liver therapy for anemia
Organizer effect in embryonic development
Prevention of tetanus
Chemical transmission of nerve impulses
Role of sinus and aortic mechanisms in regulation of respiration

Antibacterial effects of protonsil
Development of anticoagulants

1940   **Discovery of function of vitamin K**
Treatment for rheumatoid arthritis
Specific functions of nerve cells
Discovery of Rh factor
Curative effect of penicillin in bacterial infections
Prevention of diphtheria
Catalytic conversion glycogen; function of sugar in pituitary metabolism
Antibiotics
Treatment for whooping cough
Functional organization of the brain
Pump oxygenator

1950   **Antiarthritic role of adrenal hormones**
Oral diuretics for hypertension
Yellow fever vaccine
Discovery of DNA
Discovery of streptomycin
Blood preservation
Characterization of citric acid cycle
Development of open heart surgery
Culture of polio virus
Prevention of polio
Action of oxydative enzymes
Floating cardiac catheter
Cardiac pacemaker
Production of synthetic curare and its action on vascular and smooth muscle
Development of cancer chemotherapy
Discovery of chlorpromazine tranquilizers

1960   **Understanding of acquired immune intolerance**
Development of lithium
Prevention of rubella
Physical mechanism of stimulation in cochlea
Ionic involvement in excitation and inhibition in portions of the nerve
Coronary angiography
Radioimmunoassay
Defibrillation
Regulation of cholesterol and fatty acid metabolism

Cortisone
Tumor-inducing viruses and hormonal treatment of cancer
Primary physiological and chemical processes of vision
Interpretation of genetic code and its role in protein synthesis
Coronary artery bypass surgery
Cardio-pulmonary resuscitation
Corneal transplant

1970   **Mechanisms of storage and release of nerve transmitters**
Cimetadine
Mechanism of the actions of hormones
Prevention of measles
Chemical structure of antibodies
Treatment for leprosy
Organization of structural and behavioral patterns in animals
Elective cardiac arrest for surgery
Structural and functional organization of cells
Myocardial preservation
Interaction between tumor viruses and genetic material
Development of heart transplant
Slow viruses and new mechanism for dissemination of diseases
Immunotherapy
Hypothalmic hormones
Cerebral revascularization
Development of Computer Assisted Topography (CAT scans)

1980   **Identification of histocompatability antigens**
Processing of visual information by the brain
Discovery of prostaglandins
Techniques of monoclonal antibody formation
Nerve growth factor and epidermal growth factor
Basic principles of antibody synthesis
Cellular origin of retroviral oncogenes
Cyclosporin
Artificial heart

1990   **Organ transplantation techniques**
Chemical communication between cells
Laproscopic surgery
Xenotransplants

Twenty-first Century Challenges for Animal Research

cancer	birth defects
AIDS	emphysema
Alzheimer's disease	Tay-Sachs disease
Sudden Infant Death	hemophilia
Syndrome	cirrhosis
multiple sclerosis	glaucoma
muscular dystrophy	infertility
Huntington's disease	allergies
strokes	hearing impairment
head trauma	schizophrenia
spinal cord injuries	depression
paralysis	drug and alcohol addiction
Parkinson's disease	

FACT: According to an Associated Press survey, 81% of Americans support the use of animals in biomedical research. The American Medical Association reports that 97% of physicians support the use of animals in biomedical research.

Safety Testing

Whenever a new compound that may have pharmaceutical properties is synthesized, it is screened through a variety of studies using computers, cell and tissue cultures, and cadavers.

Ninety-five percent of all compounds are stopped at this level.
Only 5%, those that appear promising and not harmful, proceed to live animal tests.
Ninety-eight percent of these are stopped at this level.
Only 2% of compounds tested on live animals proceed to tests on human volunteers.
Of these, 80% are stopped at this level.

Only 20% of all compounds tested on human volunteers are approved for
distribution by the FDA.

If the live animal phase is eliminated, compounds will have to go
directly from computers, cultures, and cadavers to human trials. To bring a
pharmaceutical to distribution, we will have to do, on average, fifty times
the current number of human trials. Because people are not controlled for
genetic factors like lab rats, and because the human reproductive and life
cycles are too long to observe easily, most tests will be inferior to animal
models, and many more people will die.

APPENDIX 5

IN THEIR OWN WORDS
Quotations from Animal Rights Leaders

Anti-Humanism

- "Man is the most dangerous, destructive, selfish, and unethical animal on earth."—Michael W. Fox, vice president, Humane Society of the United States, as quoted in Robert James Bidinotto, "Animal Rights: A New Species of Egalitarianism," *The Intellectual Activist*, September 14, 1983, p. 3.
- "Mankind is the biggest blight on the face of the earth."—Ingrid Newkirk, national director, People for the Ethical Treatment of Animals, as quoted in Katie McCabe, "Beyond Cruelty," *Washingtonian*, February 1990, p. 191.
- "Humans are exploiters and destroyers, self-appointed world autocrats around whom the universe seems to revolve."—Sydney Singer, director, the Good Shepherd Foundation, "The Neediest of All Animals," *The Animals' Agenda*, Vol. 10, No. 5 (June 1990), p. 50.
- "If you haven't given voluntary human extinction much thought before, the idea of a world with no people in it may seem strange. But, if you give it a chance, I think you might agree that the extinction of Homo sapiens would mean survival for millions, if not billions, of Earth-dwelling species.... Phasing out the human race will solve every problem on earth, social and environmental."—"Les U. Knight" (pseudonym), "Voluntary Human Extinction," *Wild Earth*, Vol. 1, No. 2 (Summer 1991), p. 72.
- "Torturing a human being is almost always wrong, but it is not absolutely wrong."—Peter Singer, as quoted in Josephine Donovan, "Animal Rights and Feminist Theory," *Signs: Journal of Women in Culture and Society*, Winter 1990, p. 357.
- "I don't believe human beings have the 'right to life.' That's a supremacist perversion. A rat is a pig is a dog is a boy."—Ingrid Newkirk, national

director, People for the Ethical Treatment of Animals, as quoted in Richard Conniff, "Fuzzy-Wuzzy Thinking About Animal Rights," *Audubon*, November 1990, p. 126.

- "I find that as I get older I seem to become more of a Luddite. . . . And hearing animal experimenters describe me as a Luddite—which I used to think I was not. And now I think Ned Lud had the right idea and we should have stopped all the machinery way back when, and learned to live simple lives."—Ingrid Newkirk, national director, People for the Ethical Treatment of Animals, speech at Loyola University, October 24, 1988.

- "Back to the Pleistocene!"—Earth First! slogan, as quoted by Virginia I. Postrel, "The Green Road to Serfdom," *Reason*, April 1990, p. 24.

- "I am not a morose person, but I would rather not be here. I don't have any reverence for life, only for the entities themselves. I would rather see a blank space where I am. This will sound like fruitcake stuff again but at least I wouldn't be harming anything."—Ingrid Newkirk, national director, People for the Ethical Treatment of Animals, as quoted in Chip Brown, "She's A Portrait of Zealotry in Plastic Shoes," *Washington Post*, November 13, 1983, p. B10.

Animal Egalitarianism

- "We're not superior. There are no clear distinctions between us and animals."—Michael W. Fox, vice president, Humane Society of the United States, as quoted in Katie McCabe, "Beyond Cruelty," *Washingtonian*, February 1990, p. 192.

- "[T]here is no rational basis for maintaining a moral distinction between the treatment of humans and other animals."—The Humane Society of the United States, as quoted in Katie McCabe, "Beyond Cruelty," *Washingtonian*, February 1990, p. 192.

- "Surely there will be some nonhuman animals whose lives, by any standards, are more valuable than the lives of some humans."—Peter Singer, *Animal Liberation: A New Ethic for Our Treatment of Animals*, 2nd ed. (New York: New York Review of Books, 1990), p. 19.

- "Six million people died in concentration camps, but six billion broiler chickens will die this year in slaughterhouses."—Ingrid Newkirk, national director, People for the Ethical Treatment of Animals, as quoted in Chip Brown, "She's A Portrait of Zealotry in Plastic Shoes," *Washington Post*, November 13, 1983, p. B10.

- "Animal liberationists do not separate out the human animal, so there is no rational basis for saying that a human being has special rights. A rat is a pig is a dog is a boy. They're all mammals."—Ingrid Newkirk, national director, People for the Ethical Treatment of Animals, as quoted in Katie McCabe, "Who Will Live, Who Will Die?" *Washingtonian*, 21, No. 11 (August 1986), p. 115.
- "What could be the basis of our having more inherent value than animals? Their lack of reason, or autonomy, or intellect? Only if we are willing to make the same judgment in the case of humans who are similarly deficient."—Tom Regan, "The Case for Animal Rights," *In Defence of Animals*, Peter Singer, ed. (Oxford: Blackwell, 1985), p. 23.
- Audience member: "If you were aboard a lifeboat with a baby and a dog, and the boat capsized, would you rescue the baby or the dog?"
- Regan: "If it were a retarded baby and a bright dog, I'd save the dog."—Tom Regan, "Animal Rights, Human Wrongs," speech given at University of Wisconsin, Madison, October 27, 1989.
- "[I]f it were a child and a dog I wouldn't know for sure. . . . I might choose the human baby or I might choose the dog."—Susan Rich, outreach coordinator, People for the Ethical Treatment of Animals, on the Steve Kane Show, WIOD-AM radio, Miami, Florida, February 23, 1989.
- "If an animal researcher said, 'It's a dog or a child,' a liberator will defend the dog every time."—"Screaming Wolf" (pseudonym), *A Declaration of War: Killing People to Save Animals and the Environment* (Grass Valley, California: Patrick Henry Press, 1991), p. 14.

Biomedical Research

- "If the death of one rat cured all diseases, it wouldn't make any difference to me."—Chris DeRose, director, Last Chance for Animals, as quoted in Elizabeth Venant and David Treadwell, "Biting Back," *Los Angeles Times*, April 12, 1990, p. E12.
- "[A]n [animal] experiment cannot be justifiable unless the experiment is so important that the use of a brain-damaged human would be justifiable."—Peter Singer, *Animal Liberation: A New Ethic for Our Treatment of Animals*, 2nd ed. (New York: New York Review of Books, 1990), p. 85.
- "Even if animal tests produced a cure [for AIDS], 'we'd be against it.' "—Ingrid Newkirk, national director, People for the Ethical Treatment

of Animals, as quoted in Fred Barnes, "Politics," *Vogue*, September 1989, p. 542.

- "I do not believe that it could never be justifiable to experiment on a brain-damaged human."—Peter Singer, *Animal Liberation: A New Ethic for Our Treatment of Animals*, 2nd ed. (New York: New York Review of Books, 1990), p. 85.

- "Even painless research is fascism, supremacism, because the act of confinement is traumatizing in itself."—Ingrid Newkirk, national director, People for the Ethical Treatment of Animals, as quoted in Katie McCabe, "Who Will Live, Who Will Die?" *Washingtonian*, August 1986, p. 115.

- "[T]here could conceivably be circumstances in which an experiment on an animal stands to reduce suffering so much that it would be permissible to carry it out even if it involved harm to the animal . . . [even if] the animal were a human being."—Peter Singer, *Animal Liberation: A New Ethic for Our Treatment of Animals*, 2nd ed. (New York: New York Review of Books, 1990), p. 85.

- "I would not knowingly have an animal hurt for me, or my children, or anything else."—Cleveland Amory, founder, Fund for Animals (Larry King Show, October 29, 1987).

- "[I]n appropriate circumstances we are justified in using humans to achieve human goals (or the goal of assisting animals)."—Peter Singer, in *Behavioral and Brain Sciences* (1990, Volume 3), p. 46.

- "Never appear to be opposed to animal research; claim that your concern is only about the source of the animal used."—John McArdle, Humane Society of the United States, as quoted in Katie McCabe, "Who Will Live, Who Will Die?" *Washingtonian*, August 1986, p. 115.

- "Choose what seems most redundant, absurd, or offensive and best concentrate on cats, dogs and primates so as to ensure public sympathy."—Direct Action Paper, The Human/Animal Liberation Front, as quoted in Katie McCabe, "Who Will Live, Who Will Die?" *Washingtonian*, August 1986, p. 154.

- "If it [abolition of animal research] means there are some things we cannot learn, then so be it. We have no basic right not to be harmed by those natural diseases we are heir to."—Tom Regan, as quoted in David T. Hardy, "America's New Extremists: What You Need to Know About the Animal Rights Movement." (Washington, D.C.: Washington Legal Foundation, 1990), p. 8.

- "If natural healing is not possible, given the energy of the environment, it may be right for that being to change form. Some people call this death."— Sydney Singer, director, Good Shepherd Foundation, *The Earth Religion* (Grass Valley, California: ABACE Publications, 1991), p. 52.
- "Animal experiments occupy a central place in the material and spiritual edifice of our whole civilization. We are speaking here of one of those foundation stones whose removal could cause the whole house to collapse."—Rudolph Bahro, *Building the Green Movement*, trans. Mary Tyler (London: GMP, 1986), p. 203.

Pets

- "Pet ownership is an absolutely abysmal situation brought about by human manipulation."—Ingrid Newkirk, national director, People for the Ethical Treatment of Animals, "Just Like Us? Toward a Notion of Animal Rights" (symposium), *Harper's*, August 1988, p. 50.
- "Liberating our language by eliminating the word 'pet' is the first step. . . . In an ideal society where all exploitation and oppression has been eliminated, it will be NJARA's policy to oppose the keeping of animals as 'pets.' "—New Jersey Animal Rights Alliance, "Should Dogs Be Kept As Pets? NO!" *Good Dog!* February 1991, p. 20.
- "Let us allow the dog to disappear from our brick and concrete jungles— from our firesides, from the leather nooses and chains by which we enslave it."—John Bryant, *Fettered Kingdoms: An Examination of A Changing Ethic* (Washington, D.C.: People for the Ethical Treatment of Animals, 1982), p. 15.
- "The cat, like the dog, must disappear. . . . We should cut the domestic cat free from our dominance by neutering, neutering, and more neutering, until our pathetic version of the cat ceases to exist."—John Bryant, *Fettered Kingdoms: An Examination of A Changing Ethic* (Wahington, D.C.: People for the Ethical Treatment of Animals, 1982), p. 15.
- "As John Bryant has written in his book *Fettered Kingdoms*, they [pets] are like slaves, even if well-kept slaves."—PeTA's Statement on Companion Animals.
- "In a perfect world, all other than human animals would be free of human interference, and dogs and cats would be part of the ecological scheme."— PeTA's Statement on Companion Animals.
- "[A]s the surplus of cats and dogs (artificially engineered by centuries of

forced breeding) declined, eventually companion animals would be phased out, and we would return to a more symbiotic relationship—enjoyment at a distance."—Ingrid Newkirk, "Just Like Us? Toward a Notion of Animal Rights" (symposium), *Harper's*, August 1988, p. 50.

Agriculture

- "Meat stinks!"—People for the Ethical Treatment of Animals slogan, as quoted in Joe Vansickle, "Playing Catch-Up," *Beef*, March 1991, p. 34.
- Eating meat is "primitive, barbaric, and arrogant."—Ingrid Newkirk, national director, People for the Ethical Treatment of Animals, as quoted in Charles Griswold, Jr., "Q & A," *Washington City Paper*, December 20, 1985, p. 44.
- "My dream is that people will come to view eating an animal as cannibalism."—Henry Spira, director, Animal Rights International, as quoted in Barnaby J. Feder, "Pressuring Purdue," *New York Times Magazine*, November 26, 1989, p. 192.
- "If an animal has any rights at all, it's got the right not to be eaten."—Gary Francione, speech, University of Minnesota Law School, November 6, 1991.

Hunting

- "Hunting is an antiquated expression of macho self-aggrandizement, with no place in a civilized society."—Cleveland Amory, founder, the Fund For Animals, "They Are Bloodthirsty Nuts," *U.S. News and World Report*, February 5, 1990, p. 35.
- "[I]f we could shut down all sport hunting in a moment, we would."—Wayne Pacelle, national director, the Fund For Animals, as quoted in Bert Lindler, "Animal-Rights Activist Pacelle: 'I'm an Impassioned Agitator,' " Associated Press, December 30, 1991.
- "Many hunters are sick people. They kill beautiful animals. . . . They can invent all the excuses they want, but when you boil it all down, they want to kill something."—a spokesman for the Committee to Abolish Sport Hunting, as quoted in William G. Tapply, "Who Speaks for People?" *Field & Stream*, June 1991, p. 48.
- "These bloodthirsty nuts claim they provide a service for the environment. Nonsense! A hunter goes into the woods to kill something, period."—Cleveland Amory, founder, the Fund For Animals, "They

Are Bloodthirsty Nuts," *U.S. News and World Report*, February 5, 1990, p. 35.

- "Having hunters oversee wildlife is like having Dracula guard the blood bank."—Wayne Pacelle, national director, the Fund For Animals, as quoted in William G. Tapply, "Who Speaks for People?" *Field & Stream*, June 1991, p. 48.

- "We want to stigmatize hunting, we see it as the next logical target and we believe it is vulnerable."—Wayne Pacelle, national director, the Fund For Animals, as quoted in William G. Tapply, "Who Speaks for People?" *Field & Stream*, June 1991, p. 48.

Animal Welfare vs. Animal Rights

- "The theory of animal rights simply is not consistent with the theory of animal welfare. . . . Animal rights means dramatic social changes for humans and non-humans alike; if our bourgeois values prevent us from accepting those changes, then we have no right to call ourselves advocates of animal rights."—Gary Francione, *The Animals' Voice*, Vol. 4, No. 2 (undated), pp. 54–55.

- "Not only are the philosophies of animal rights and animal welfare separated by irreconcilable differences . . . the enactment of animal welfare measures actually impedes the achievement of animal rights. . . . [W]elfare reforms, by their very nature, can only serve to retard the pace at which animal rights goals are achieved."—Gary Francione and Tom Regan, "A Movement's Means Create Its Ends," *The Animals' Agenda*, January/February 1992, pp. 40–42.

- "The major success of this decade [the 1980s] has been the reapplication of the concept of rights in the human population to nonhuman species."—John Kullberg, president, American Society for the Prevention of Cruelty to Animals, as quoted in Charles Oliver, "Liberation Zoology," *Reason*, 22, No. 2 (June 1990), p. 24.

- "We were not especially 'interested in' animals. Neither of us had ever been inordinately fond of dogs, cats, or horses in the way that many people are. We didn't 'love' animals."—Peter Singer, *Animal Liberation: A New Ethic for Our Treatment of Animals*, 2nd ed. (New York: New York Review of Books, 1990), Preface, p. ii.

ENDNOTES

Introduction

1. The logo of People for the Ethical Treatment of Animals has a lower case *e* for *ethical*, and we have followed the organization's lead. We think that the small *e* is appropriate since PeTA's ethics are lower case, too.
2. Harry R. Hueston II, "Terrorism in the '90s: Battling the Animal Liberation Front,"*Police Chief*, September 1990, p. 52.
3. Ibid.
4. President Bill Clinton has since named his economic program "Putting People First." This program has nothing to do with our organization, and Putting People First has no relationship with the president or any of his legislation. We asked Mr. Clinton, when he was a candidate, to stop using our name, but he refused. In 1993, the Trademark Office registered Putting People First as our trademark.

Chapter 1

1. Peter Singer, *Animal Liberation: A New Ethic for Our Treatment of Animals*, 2nd ed. (New York: New York Review of Books, 1990), p. 19. Singer concludes that "an [animal] experiment cannot be justifiable unless the experiment is so important that the use of a brain-damaged human would be justifiable." (p. 85); "I do not believe that it could never be justifiable to experiment on a brain-damaged human." (Ibid.); "Torturing a human being is almost always wrong, but it is not absolutely wrong." (Ibid.); "[T]here could conceivably be circumstances in which an experiment on an animal stands to reduce suffering so much that it would be permissable to carry it out even if it involved harm to the animal ... [even if] the animal were a human being." (Peter Singer, as quoted in Josephine Donovan, "Animal Rights

and Feminist Theory," *Signs: Journal of Women in Culture and Society*, Winter 1990, p. 357); "[I]n appropriate circumstances we are justified in using humans to achieve human goals (or the goal of assisting animals)." (Peter Singer, in *Behavioral and Brain Sciences* [1990, Volume 3, pp. 1–60], p. 46); "[P]arents should be allowed, in consultation with their doctors, to make life and death decisions for their severely disabled newborn infants. When a decision has been made that it is better for a severely disabled newborn infant to die ... I consider that the use of active means of bringing about death may be preferable to a long, drawn out and distressing period of dying." (Peter Singer, as quoted by Carla Bennet, PeTA, in letter, "A Diabolical Distortion of an Ethicist's Position," *Washington Times*, February 7, 1992). Cf. Peter Singer and Helga Kuhse, *Should the Baby Live? The Problem of Defective Infants* (Oxford, England: Oxford Univ. Press, 1985).

2. Tom Regan, "The Case for Animal Rights," *In Defence of Animals*, Peter Singer, ed. (Oxford: Blackwell, 1985), p. 23.

3. Tom Regan, "Animal Rights, Human Wrongs," speech given at University of Wisconsin, Madison, October 27, 1989.

4. "[PeTA National Director Ingrid] Newkirk says that even if animal tests produced a cure [for AIDS], 'we'd be against it.' " (Quoted in Fred Barnes, "Politics," *Vogue*, September 1989, p. 542); "If the death of one rat cured all diseases, it wouldn't make any difference to me." (Chris DeRose, director, Last Chance for Animals, quoted in Elizabeth Venant and David Treadwell, "Biting Back," *Los Angeles Times*, April 12, 1990, p. E12); "If it [abolition of animal research] means there are some things we cannot learn, then so be it. We have no basic right not to be harmed by those natural diseases we are heir to." (Tom Regan, quoted in David T. Hardy, "America's New Extremists: What You Need to Know About the Animal Rights Movement" [Washington, D.C.: Washington Legal Foundation, 1990], p. 8); "If natural healing is not possible, given the energy of the environment, it may be right for that being to change form. Some people call this death." (Sydney Singer, director, Good Shepherd Foundation, *The Earth Religion* [Grass Valley, California: ABACE Publications, 1991], p. 52).

5. Cf. Tom Regan, "The Case for Animal Rights," *In Defence of Animals*, Peter Singer, ed. (Oxford: Blackwell, 1985), p. 13; "We even oppose the use of honey, because bees die in the process of gathering it." (Carol L. Burnett, PeTA communications director, *Marin Independent Journal*, June 25, 1989); "Every year, millions of cows, sheep, goats and pigs are

slaughtered for their flesh and skin." (*PeTA News*, May / June 1989); "Our society is based on by-products. They don't create the meat industry; the meat industry creates them. Giving up leather is not really going to be the issue. It's going to be giving up the meat industry." (Doll Stanley, "In Defense of Animals," *Oakland Tribune*, February 11, 1990); "That's [leather] the next step. You have to take one step at a time. It was easier to start with fur." (Dan Matthews, PeTA director of international campaigns, *Detroit News*, August 13, 1989); "Never buy wool again." (*PeTA News*, op. cit); "[A]nyone who has plucked her eyebrows can imagine how painful it is for some geese who are raised for down to have all their feathers pulled from their breasts or necks." Ibid. [Note: down is shed naturally, and live fowl are not plucked for feathers.]; Silkworms "are steamed or boiled alive by the thousands in silk production . . . and it is now a well-established biological fact that silkworms feel pain." (Ibid).

6. "Eventually companion animals would be phased out. . . ." Ingrid Newkirk, "Just Like Us? Toward a Notion of Animal Rights" (symposium), *Harper's*, August 1988. See chapter 6.

7. "I'm against using guide dogs." (Kathy Guillermo, PeTA compassion campaign director, on "Speak Your Mind with Howie Green," WHFS radio, Annapolis, Maryland, August 11, 1991); "[I]n a perfect society we won't have a need for that [guide dogs]. . . ." (Ingrid Newkirk, as quoted in Charles Griswold, Jr., "Q & A," *Washington City Paper*, December 20, 1985, p. 44); cf. David Zimmerman, "Animal Activists Hassle The Blind, Claiming Guide Dogs Are Abused," *Probe*, February 1, 1993, pp. 6–8; "A member of FORWARD Working Dog Support Group, made up of guide-dog handlers and friends, was harassed and physically threatened" by an "animal rights activist." (Jenine McKeown, former president of the Columbus, Ohio, chapter of the American Council of the Blind, *Columbus Dispatch*, December 24, 1991.)

8. Gary Francione, *The Animals' Voice*, Vol. 4, No. 2 (undated), pp. 54–55.

9. Gary Francione and Tom Regan, "A Movement's Means Create Its Ends," *The Animals' Agenda*, January / February 1992, pp. 40–42.

10. Peter Singer (1990), op. cit., Preface, p. ii.

11. Richard Conniff, "Fuzzy-Wuzzy Thinking About Animal Rights," *Audubon*, November 1990, p. 126; "I don't believe that human beings have 'the right to life'. . . . This 'right to human life' I believe is another perversion." (Newkirk, in Griswold, op. cit., p. 48); "Animal

liberationists do not separate out the human animal, so there is no rational basis for saying that a human being has special rights. A rat is a pig is a dog is a boy. They're all mammals." (Newkirk, in Katie McCabe, "Who Will Live, Who Will Die?" *Washingtonian*, 21, No. 11 [August 1986] p. 115); Cf. Barnes, op. cit.; and John G. Hubbell, "The 'Animal Rights' War on Medicine," *Reader's Digest*, June 1990, p. 72. After receiving criticism for this statement, Newkirk rephrased it as *"When it comes to feelings*, a rat is a pig is a dog is a boy." Now she uses the latter assertion to claim that her words were misquoted or taken out of context. But she refuses to retract the original version.

12. "Humans differentiate kinds or classes of which there are no perceptual instances in their experience or of which there cannot be any. This is the distinguishing characteristic of conceptual thought and the irrefutable evidence of the presence of intellect in man and its absence in brutes." Mortimer J. Adler, *Ten Philosophical Mistakes* (New York: Macmillan, 1985), p. 76.

13. For the classical view of moral responsibilities, see Aristotle, *Ethics*, trans. J.A.K. Thomson (New York: Penguin Classics, 1985), pp. 111–141.

14. Barnes, op. cit.

15. Griswold, op. cit., p. 37. Cf. Hubbell, op. cit; and McCabe (1990), p. 191: "Mankind is the biggest blight on the face of the earth."

16. Chip Brown, "She's A Portrait of Zealotry in Plastic Shoes," *Washington Post*, November 13, 1983, p. B10.

17. McCabe (1990), p. 192.

18. Michael W. Fox, *Returning to Eden*, quoted in Robert James Bidinotto, "Animal Rights: A New Species of Egalitarianism," *Intellectual Activist*, September 14, 1983, p. 3.

19. Troy Mader, "The Enemy Within," *Abundant Wildlife*, September 1992, p. 4.

20. Sydney Singer, "The Neediest of All Animals," *The Animals' Agenda*, Vol. 10, No. 5 (June 1990), p. 50.

21. "Screaming Wolf" (pseudonym), *A Declaration of War: Killing People to Save Animals and the Environment* (Grass Valley, California: Patrick Henry Press, 1991).

22. "Les U. Knight" (pseudonym), "Voluntary Human Extinction," *Wild Earth*, Vol. 1, No. 2 (Summer 1991), p. 72.

23. Brown (1983), op. cit.

Chapter 2

1. "The FBI now lists the ALF as one of the 10 most dangerous terrorist organizations." "Technology Against Terrorism: Structuring Security," Congress of the United States, Office of Technology Assessment (Washington, D.C.: Government Printing Office, January 1992), p. 26.

2. Jack Rosenberger, "The Ugly Secret of Black Beauty Ranch," *Village Voice*, December 18, 1990, pp. 39–42.

3. "Animal Rights Advocate Arrested in Bomb Planting in Connecticut," *New York Times*, November 12, 1988; "Woman in Bomb Case Gets 3-Year Probation," *New York Times*, January 9, 1990.

4. Ellen Hopkins, "Animal Rights," *Newsday*, February 21, 1988, p. 24.

5. Leslie Spencer with Jan Bollwerk and Richard C. Morais, "The Not So Peaceful World of Greenpeace," *Forbes*, November 11, 1991, pp. 174–180.

6. *Survival in the High North* asserted that Greenpeace used "falsifications," that the "scene which was shown was without doubt falsified," and that Greenpeace "exploited" the "myth" that "the hunter skins the seals while they are still alive." Greenpeace sued Gudmundsson for libel in March 1992, after his film was broadcast on Norwegian television. On May 27, 1992, the Oslo Municipal court ruled that these assertions were not libelous. (Tim Oliver, " 'Greenpeace Falsified the Evidence,' " *Fishing News* [London], June 5, 1992.) Bjorn Okern, chairman of Greenpeace Norway, resigned, calling the organization "ecofascist." Greenpeace's Norwegian and Danish membership consequently plummeted from 15,000 to 35, and on September 24, 1992, *21st Century Science and Technology* reported that Greenpeace International had decided to shut down its Norwegian operations. One wonders what would happen if this documentary were aired on PBS.

7. Cf. Janice Henke, *Seal Wars! An American Viewpoint* (St. John's, Newfoundland: Breakwater Books Ltd., 1985).

8. John Lancaster, "The Green Guerrilla," *Washington Post*, March 20, 1991, p. B1.

9. "Betsy Swart, PeTA's secretary, is also affiliated with Friends of Animals and In Defense of Animals; Susan Brebner, who heads up education at PeTA, is in charge of National Association of Nurses Against Vivisection; Dr. Neal Barnard (who maintained a desk at PeTA in earlier years) leads the Physicians Committee for Responsible Medicine and serves as a director on the board of New England Anti-Vivisection Society . . . ,"

Rod and Patti Strand, *The Hijacking of the Humane Movement* (Wilsonville, Oregon: Doral Publishing, 1992), pp. 51–52.

10. Lee Wallot, "The Wrongs of Animal Activism and How They Affect You," *Sheltie International*, February 1993, p. 52.

11. Charles Oliver, "Liberation Zoology," *Reason*, 22, No. 2 (June 1990), p. 24.

12. Elisabeth Hickey, "Going to the Dogs? The ASPCA Joins the Animal Rights Movement," *Washington Times*, October 12, 1990, p. E8.

13. "The Humane Society of the United States is a nationally known organization that practices animal rights while collecting mainstream contributions from an unsuspecting public." Strand, op. cit., p. 60.

14. Katie McCabe, "Beyond Cruelty," *Washingtonian*, 25, No. 5 (February 1990), p. 192.

15. Ron Arnold and Alan Gottlieb, *Trashing the Economy: How Runaway Environmentalism Is Wrecking America* (Bellevue, Washington: Free Enterprise Press, 1993), p. 274.

16. HSUS "Holiday Fundraising Appeal," McCabe (1990), p. 192.

17. The number may be much higher: "The 1992 figures show more than 400 animal rights groups with 990 IRS forms displaying the total budgets for 26 most active and visible animal protection, welfare and rights groups at $577 million." Strand, op. cit., p. 55.

18. "Animal Activism: The New Pornography," *Who's Mailing What!* Stamford, Connecticut: The Direct Marketing Archive, Vol. 6, Nos. 10 & 11 (July/August 1990), p. 21. See also Charles S. Nicholl, "In Defense of Animals Maligns Universities, Scientists," *West County Times* (Richmond, California), May 22, 1991, p. 9B.

19. Jack Anderson and Joseph Spear, "Where Charity Begins at the Top," *Washington Post*, October 13, 1988, p. DC13.

20. Jack Anderson and Dale Van Atta, "Questions on Humane Society Finances," *Washington Post*, February 20, 1991, p. D16.

21. *Who's Mailing What!* op. cit., p. 1.

22. Rebecca T. Richards and Richard S. Krannich, "The Ideology of the Animal Rights Movement and Activists' Attitudes Toward Wildlife." (unpublished paper)

23. Wesley V. Jamison and William Lunch, "A Preliminary Report: Results from Demographic, Attitudinal, and Behavioral Analysis of the Animal Rights Movement." (unpublished paper) Cf. Wesley V. Jamison and William Lunch, "Rights of Animals, Perceptions of Science, and Political Activism: Profile of Animal Rights Activists," *Science, Technology, and Human Values*, Vol. 17 (Autumn 1992), pp. 438–458.

24. Ibid. Also see "Survey Shows Movement Promise," *The Animals' Agenda*, March 1991, p. 2; and Marlys Miller, "Who Are the Real Animal Activists?" and "High-Income Females Fill Rightists Ranks," *Pork '91*, July 1991, p. 31.

Chapter 3

1. Ron Arnold and Alan Gottlieb, *Trashing the Economy: How Runaway Environmentalism Is Wrecking America* (Bellevue, Washington: Free Enterprise Press, 1993), p. 416. See also Rod and Patti Strand, *The Hijacking of the Humane Movement* (Wilsonville, Oregon: Doral Publishing, 1991), p. 48.

2. A fellow scientist has stated: "In addition to his landmark studies of the recuperative potential of damaged nervous sytems, Dr. Taub's contributions to the relatively new discipline of biofeedback have vast and immediate therapeutic implications in such diverse areas as psychiatry, neurology, cardiology, and gastroenterology. . . . [I]n fact, to speak merely of his 'contributions' is to minimize his efforts, as Dr. Taub is actually one of the founding fathers of this field." *Baltimore Sun*, November 11, 1981, as quoted in Hamilton D. Moore, Brief of Amicus Curiae, *Berosini v. PeTA*, note 5, pp. 13–14.

3. Edward Taub, "The Silver Spring Monkey Incident: The Untold Story," *Coalition For Animals & Animal Research Newsletter*, Vol. 4, No. 1 (Winter/Spring 1991), p. 3.

4. Peter Carlson, "The Great Silver Spring Monkey Debate," *Washington Post Magazine*, February 24, 1991, p. 18. This reversal was based on limitations of the Maryland law; the appellate court did not get to the issue of whether Dr. Taub abused his monkeys.

5. Susan Okie and Veronica Jennings, "'Rescued' Animals Killed," *Washington Post*, April 13, 1991, pp. A1, A9.

6. "Fact Sheet: 'Silver Spring Monkeys,'" National Institutes of Health, June 20, 1991. See also *Science*, June 28, 1991.

7. George Bennett, "PeTA Kills 'Rescued' Animals," *Montgomery County* [Maryland] *Journal*, April 14, 1991, p. A1.

8. U.S. Congressman Vin Weber, press release, April 15, 1991.

9. "A Very Special Place," *PeTA Kids*, No. 3 (Summer 1989), p. 6.

10. Deposition of Sam Alston, 27, 34–52, *Berosini v. PeTA*. Case No. A276505 (District Ct., Clark County, Nevada).

11. Deposition of Gary Thorud, 58, *Berosini v. PeTA*.

12. David Arnold, "Fight Looms over Animal Rights Group," *Boston Globe*, April 10, 1987, p. 23.

13. Ibid.

14. Alex Pacheco with Anna Francione, "The Silver Spring Monkeys," *In Defence of Animals*, Peter Singer, ed. (Oxford: Blackwell, 1985), p. 135.

15. Chip Brown, "She's a Portrait of Zealotry in Plastic Shoes, *Washington Post*, November 13, 1983, p. B10.

16. Charles Griswold, Jr., "Q & A," *Washington City Paper*, December 20, 1985, p. 44.

17. PeTA Factsheet, Miscellaneous #5, "The Animal Liberation Front: Army of the Kind," (Washington, D.C.: People for the Ethical Treatment of Animals, 1993).

18. Deposition of Alex Pacheco, *Berosini v. PeTA*, pp. 61–62.

19. *Berosini v. PeTA*, Exhibit 9.

20. "Activism and the Law: A Legal Primer," (Washington, D.C.: People for the Ethical Treatment of Animals, undated).

21. Ibid.

22. Personal communication from Dr. Orem. See also John Orem, "Obstacles to Inquiry," *The People's Agenda*, February 1991, p. 6.

23. "NIH Report Clears Texas Tech," *NABR* (National Association for Biomedical Research) *Update*, 11, No. 10 (March 23, 1990), p. 1. See also Arnold and Gottlieb, op. cit., pp. 412–13.

24. *PeTA Catalog*, p. 27 (*Berosini v. PeTA*, exhibit 14).

25. "Animal Rights Group Ransacks Professor's Office at Vet School," *The Daily Pennsylvanian*, January 15, 1990, p. A4. Cf. "Guerrillas Monkey With Vet Prof's Work," and "Animal Rights Guerillas Trash Professor's Office," both from *Philadelphia Daily News*, January 15, 1990.

26. "University of Pennsylvania Head Injury Laboratory," *Animal Legal Defense Fund Newsletter* No. 1 (1986), p. 2. Cf. letter from William F. Raub, Ph.D., deputy director of the U.S. Department of Health and Human Services, National Institutes of Health, July 8, 1989.

27. Jerry W. Byrd, "Two Sides Meet at Animal Research Rally," *Philadelphia Inquirer*, February 4, 1990, p. 2B.

28. Jack Rosenberger, "Animal Rites," *Village Voice*, March 6, 1990, p. 34.

29. "PeTA Smells a Lot of Bologna," *PeTA News*, September/October 1990, p. 26. Cf. Letter from Ann Chynoweth, PeTA, May 8, 1990, *Berosini v. PeTA*, Exhibit 18.

30. ALF left a note at the scene explaining its rationale for destroying equipment: vandalism drains money from research budgets: "[T]he $10,000 microscope was destroyed in about ten seconds with a steel wrecking bar purchased for less than $5. We consider that a pretty good return. . . . [T]he damage we cause represents money unavailable for the purchase, mutilation and slaughter of animals." McCabe (1990), p. 186.
31. Deposition of Gary Thorud, *Berosini v. PeTA*, at 49–50.
32. Deposition of Sam Alston, 27, 34–52, *Berosini v. PeTA*.
33. Michael Satchell, "Pursuing PeTA," *U.S. News and World Report*, September 21, 1992, p. 19.
34. Fund-raising letter (1992, undated), People for the Ethical Treatment of Animals.

Chapter 4

1. Larry King Show, October 29, 1987.
2. Lawrence K. Altman, "Man Given Baboon's Liver in Transplant 'Doing Well,' Doctors Say," *New York Times*, July 1, 1992, p. A18.
3. Suzanne E. Roy (public affairs director, In Defense of Animals), Letter, *New York Times*, July 16, 1992, p. A24.
4. "Recipient of Baboon Liver Awake, Alert," *Washington Post*, June 30, 1992, p. A3.
5. Sally Squires, "Organs from Animals," *Washington Post Health*, July 14, 1992, p. 9.
6. Alice Steinbach, "Whose Life Is an Animal's or a Child's?" *Glamour*, January 1990, p. 173.

   Alternatively, animal activists attempt to deny that animal models have been useful in developing insulin, as in Brandon Reines, *The Truth Behind the Discovery of Insulin* (Jenkintown, Pennsylvania: American Anti-Vivisection Society, 1985). For a different perspective, see Michael Bliss, *The Discovery of Insulin* (Chicago: University of Chicago Press, 1982), p. 13. For an overview of the controversy, see Ernest Verhetsel, *They Threaten Your Health*, 2nd ed. (Washington, D.C.: Putting People First, 1992), pp. 65–69.
7. Or claim vaccines actually cause net harm: "I believe that we're now beginning to learn—and many people are stopping to vaccinate their children—that we have wreaked havoc on our immune system by

such a dependency on such an animal-based vaccine in our youth. We have injected animal proteins into our bodies that have lain dormant for years and are now perhaps crossing the species barrier and doing all sorts of things. . . ." Ingrid Newkirk, as quoted in Charles Griswold, Jr., "Q & A," *City Paper*, December 20, 1985, p. 44.

8. "The International Union of Physiological Sciences," *Coalition for Animals and Animal Research Newsletter*, 2, No. 3 (Fall 1989), p. 17.

9. Foundation for Biomedical Research *Newsletter*, VIII, No. 1, undated, pp. 3–4.

10. Cf. Ronald Melzack and Patrick D. Wall, *The Challenge of Pain: Exciting Discoveries in the New Science of Pain Control*, rev. ed. (New York: Basic Books, 1983). A concise discussion of the issues can be found in "Claude Skatole" (pseudonym), ed., *The Garbage Collector*, Vol. 3, No. 11, 1990, p. 5.

11. "U.S. Food and Drug Administration Position Paper: Animal Use in Testing FDA-regulated Products," October 7, 1992.

12. Cosmetics, Toiletries and Fragrances Association (CTFA), Information kit.

13. Ibid.

14. Letter from Gerald B. Guest to Hon. John S. Arnick, chairman, Judiciary Committee, Maryland House of Delegates, Annapolis, May 13, 1991.

15. Gary Hofing, "Briefings from the Michigan Society for Medical Research," October 5, 1991.

16. CTFA, op. cit.

17. Ibid.

18. Ibid.

19. Letter from Alan Goldberg to John Arnick, chairman, Judiciary Committee, Maryland House of Delegates, Annapolis, February 27, 1991.

20. Conversation with Benjamin Trump, May 15, 1991.

21. The Body Shop, "Animals in Danger" (Pamphlet #04038), Cedar Knolls, N.J., August 1992.

22. Ibid. (Pamphlet #4249).

23. As quoted in John G. Hubbell, "The Animal Rights War on Medicine," *Reader's Digest*, 136, No. 818 (June 1990), p. 72.

24. PeTA Factsheet, "Animal Experiments," Washington, D.C.: People for the Ethical Treatment of Animals, 1993.

25. Steve Carroll, "M.D. versus M.D.," *iiFARsighted Report*, Incurably Ill for Animal Research, 4, No. 1 (Winter 1990), p. 6.

26. Andrew A. Skolnick, "AMA Asked to Seek Protection for Researchers from Political Interference by Animal Activists," *Journal of the American Medical Association*, 266, No. 4 (July 24, 1991), p. 466.

27. "Congress Continues Suspension of Two DoD Projects," *NABR Update*, National Association for Biomedical Research, 11, No. 34 (December 21, 1990), p. 1.

28. Skolnick, op. cit.

29. Charles W. Plows, letter to Neal Barnard, *CFAAR Newsletter* (Coalition for Animals and Animal Research), Winter/Spring 1991, p. 34.

30. Ibid. See Resolution 109, 1990 House Delegates Report, American Medical Association; "AMA Refutes Validity of 'Physicians Group' Report," AMA News Release, April 11, 1991; Roy M. Schwartz, "AMA Blasts Animal Rights Group on Milk Panic," September 29, 1992; James S. Todd, Letter to Neal Barnard, July 26, 1990; *Information Digest*, May 5, 1991, p. 10; Adrian R. Morrison, "Letter to the Montgomery Journal," *CFAAR Newsletter* (Coalition for Animals and Animal Research), Summer/Fall 1991, pp. 33–34.

31. "There is virtually no major treatment or surgical procedure in modern medicine that could have been developed without animal research." Robert J. White, "The Facts About Animal Research," *Reader's Digest*, March 1988, p. 127.

32. Katie McCabe, "Beyond Cruelty," *Washingtonian*, 25, No. 5 (February 1990), p. 194.

33. "Action for Animals: A Rising Tide," Animal Rights Coalition Conference (ARCC), September 27–29, 1985.

34. Barbara F. Orlans, "Debating Dissection," *The Science Teacher*, November 1988, p. 38.

35. Thomas R. Lord, "The Importance of Animal Dissection," *Journal of College Science Teaching*, May 1990, p. 330. Cf. also John Richard Schrock, "Dissection," *The Kansas School Naturalist*, Vol. 36, No. 3 (February 1990), reprint, 16 pp.

36. Steve Weinberg, "A Message from the President of Educators for Responsible Science" (Westport, Connecticut).

37. "Animal Rights in America's Classroom," *Foundation for Biomedical Research Newsletter*, Vol. 6, No. 6.

38. Constance Holden, "Animal Rights Activism Threatens Dissection," *Science*, 250 (November 9, 1990), p. 9.

39. Katie McCabe, "Who Will Live, Who Will Die?" *Washingtonian*, 21, No. 11 (August 1986), p. 115.

40. "Action for Animals," op. cit.
41. "Issues and Answers," incurably ill For Animal Research, Bridgeview, Illinois (undated), p. 10.
42. Christopher Meyers, "People for the Ethical Treatment of Animals, 325,000 Strong, Assumes Influential, Controversial Role in Fierce National Battle," *Chronicle of Higher Education*, November 10, 1990.
43. Media General-Associated Press opinion poll, cited in "Join the Majority and Support Animal Research," incurably ill For Animal Research (undated).
44. American Medical Association, "Survey of Physicians Attitudes Toward the Use of Animals in Biomedical Research" (Chicago, Illinois: American Medical Association, 1989). See also Council Report, "Use of Animals in Medical Education," *Journal of the American Medical Association*, 266, No. 4 (August 14, 1991), p. 836.
45. McCabe, 1986, op. cit.
46. "The International Union of Physiological Sciences," *Coalition for Animals and Animal Research Newsletter*, 2, No. 3 (Fall 1989), p. 17.
47. Retha Hill, "Protestors Stalk Researcher over Cat Experiments," *Washington Post*, June 23, 1991, p. C6.
48. "[N]o one, unless he is grossly ignorant of what science has done for mankind, can entertain any doubt of the incalculable benefits which hereafter will be derived from physiology, not only by man, but by the lower animals. Look for instance at Pasteur's results in modifying the germs of the most malignant diseases, from which, as it so happens, animals will in the first place receive more relief than man." Charles Darwin, letter to Frithiof Holingren (professor of physiology at Upsala), printed in *London Times*, April 18, 1881. From *Life and Letters of Charles Darwin*, Vol. III (London: Murray, 1888). From the same letter: "[P]hysiology cannot possibly progress except by means of experiments on living animals, and ... he who retards the progress of physiology commits a crime against mankind." Thus Darwin himself contradicts Peter Singer's assertion that Darwinism makes animal research immoral.
49. Alan M. Goldberg and John M. Frazier, "Alternatives to Animals in Toxicity Testing," *Scientific American*, 261, No. 2 (August 1989), p. 24.
50. "Animal Rights Raiders Destroy Years of Work," *New York Times*, Campus Life, March 8, 1992.

51. Erin Marcus, "New Research Methods Seen Unlikely to Eliminate Animal Testing," *Washington Post*, August 28, 1990, p. A3.
52. Philip E. Ross, "Man's Best Friend," *Scientific American*, 265, No. 2 (August 1991), p. 28.
53. "The International Union of Physiological Sciences," *Coalition for Animals and Animal Research Newsletter*, 2, No. 3 (Fall 1989), p. 17.
54. R. E. Burke, "Computer Models in Biomedical Research," *Animal Care Matters*, August 1989, p. 4.
55. McCabe (1986), p. 116.
56. As quoted in *Cable Guide*, April 1990, pp. 32–33.
57. Council Report, "Use of Animals in Medical Education," *Journal of the American Medical Association*, 266, No. 4 (August 14, 1991), p. 836.
58. Ibid.
59. Barbara Brotman, "Building a Resistance," *Chicago Tribune*, November 2, 1990, p. 8.
60. Ibid.
61. Andrew A. Skolnick, "Terrorists Strike Again as U.S. Congress Considers Bills to Outlaw Attacks on Animal Research Centers," *Journal of the American Medical Association*, 267, No. 19 (May 20, 1992), p. 2578.
62. David T. Hardy, "America's New Extremists: What You Need to Know About the Animal Rights Movement," Washington: D.C.: Washington Legal Foundation, 1990, p. 34.
63. Joyce Price, "Animal Activists Threaten Studies," *Washington Times*, March 3, 1990, p. A1. Cf. *Washington Times*, March 5, 1990, p. A10.
64. W. Raymond Wannall, "Silence Over Animal Rights Violence," *Washington Times*, August 20, 1991, p. G3.
65. Fred Barnes, "Politics," *Vogue*, September 1989, p. 542.
66. Elizabeth Venant and David Treadwell, "Biting Back," *Los Angeles Times*, April 12, 1990, p. E12.
67. Tom Regan, *The Case for Animal Rights* (1983), quoted in McCabe (1990), p. 193. See also Hardy, op. cit., p. 8.
68. Ingrid Newkirk, speech at Loyola University, October 24, 1988.
69. Rudolph Bahro, *Building the Green Movement*, trans. Mary Tyler (London: GMP, 1986), p. 203.
70. Ibid.
71. Sydney Singer, *The Earth Religion* (Grass Valley, California: ABACE Publications, 1991), p. 52.

Chapter 5

1. See Debbie Howlett, "Ad Links Animal Slaughter, Dahmer Case," *USA Today*, August 9, 1991, p. 3A.
2. For a concise discussion of the misconceptions of animal rights regarding the treatment of domesticated animals, see Stephen Budianski, *The Covenant of the Wild* (New York: William Morrow and Company, 1992), pp. 148–150.
3. Mitchell Davis, "The Foie Gras Factor," *New York Times*, May 25, 1992, p. 19.
4. "Anti-Beaking Concession," *Pennsylvanians for Responsible Use of Animals Newsletter*, 1, No. 1 (Spring 1990).
5. "Network Notes," *Animals' Agenda*, Vol. 9, No. 9 (December 1989), p. 12.
6. *Washington Times*, December 6, 1991, p. A12.
7. John Robbins, *Diet for a New America* (Walpole, N.H.: Stillpoint, 1987), pp. 352–363.
8. Stephan Bodian, "Diet for a New America: An Interview with Stephen Bodian," *Yoga Journal*, September/October 1988. Cf. John Robbins, "Rebel With a Cause," *New Age Journal*, May/June 1988.
9. Jeremy Rifkin, *Beyond Beef: The Rise and Fall of the Cattle Culture* (New York: Dutton, 1992).
10. Jack Rosenberger, "The Ugly Secret of Black Beauty Ranch," *Village Voice*, December 18, 1990, pp. 39–42.
11. Carole Sugarman, "Beefing about the American Diet," *Washington Post*, April 28, 1992, p. 12.
12. Ibid.
13. Robert S. Chapkin, "Meat and Chronic Disease," in *Current Issues in Food Production: A Perspective on Beef as a Component in Diets for Americans*, H. Russell Cross and Floyd M. Byers, ed. (College Station: Texas A & M University, April 1990), pp. 12.1–12.16.
14. Marian Burros, "Cow's Milk and Children: A New No-No?" *New York Times*, September 30, 1992, p. C1.
15. Carole Sugarman, "No Use Crying over Spilt Milk," *Washington Post*, October 7, 1992, p. E1.
16. Isadore Rosenfeld, "Milk Under Attack," *Vogue*, Vol. 183, No. 3 (March 1993), p. 276.
17. F. M. Byers, "Chemicals in the Meat Supply: A Review," in Cross and Byers, ed., op. cit., p. 10.5.

18. "In the U.S. system, only 39% of the total energy and 20% of the total plant protein are recovered from a crop of corn whereas by using the residual of the plants and the bran (removal of outer coating) of the grain following human food preparation as animal feed, subsistence farms effectively recuperate 51% of the energy and 30% of the protein from their planting of corn." R. E. McDowell, *A Partnership for Humans and Animals* (Raleigh, N.C.: Kinnic Publishers, 1991), p. 12.

19. Alston Chase, "Ending Grazing Won't Save the Range," *Grand Forks* (North Dakota) *Herald*, August 12, 1991, p. 4A.

20. "Absence of Evidence for Greenhouse Warming over the Arctic Ocean in the Past 40 Years," *Nature*, January 28, 1993.

21. Cf. Ronald Bailey, "Captain Planet for Veep," *National Review*, September 14, 1992, p. 45.

22. Cf. Dixy Lee Ray and Lou Guzzo, *Environmental Overkill: Whatever Happened to Common Sense?* (Washington, D.C.: Regnery Gateway, 1993), p. 15.

23. Dixy Lee Ray with Lou Guzzo, *Trashing the Planet: How Science Can Help Us Deal with Acid Rain, Depletion of the Ozone, and Nuclear Waste (Among Other Things)* (Washington, D.C., Regnery Gateway, 1990), p. 33.

24. "History of Animal Rights Extremism," *Animal Rights Reporter*, Vol. 1, No. 6 (April 1989), pp. 10–17; Vol. 1, No. 7 (May 1989), pp. 3–4; Vol. 1, No. 8 (June 1989), p. 15; Vol. 1, No. 9 (July 1989), pp. 10–11; Vol. 1, No. 10 (August 1989), pp. 5–6; Vol. 2, No. 12 (June 1, 1990), p. 4. See also "Animal Rights Movement Activities Summary, United States," Foundation for Biomedical Research (undated).

25. Ibid.

26. John S. Miller, "Saboteurs Step Up Nevada Ranch Attacks," *Reno Gazette Journal*, November 21, 1989, p. 1A.

Chapter 6

1. Cole McFarland, "At Our Service," *The Animals' Agenda*, Vol. 3, No. 2, p. 28.

2. Jenine McKeown, *Columbus Dispatch*, December 24, 1991. See also David Zimmerman, "Animal Activists Hassle The Blind, Claiming Guide Dogs Are Abused," *Probe*, February 1, 1993, pp. 6–8. Cf. Charles Griswold, Jr., "Q & A," *City Paper*, December 20, 1985, p. 44.

3. J. Tevere MacFadyen, "Monkeys with Helping Hands," *Reader's Digest*, October 1987, p. 7.

4. Mark Vosburgh, "Monkey Project for Disabled Puts Disney in Tough Spot," *Orlando Sentinel*, March 3, 1990, p. D7.

5. "Statement on Companion Animals," People for the Ethical Treatment of Animals, undated.

6. John Bryant, *Fettered Kingdoms: An Examination of a Changing Ethic* (Washington, D.C.: People for the Ethical Treatment of Animals, 1982), p. 15.

7. Ingrid Newkirk, "Just Like Us? Toward a Notion of Animal Rights," (symposium) *Harper's*, August 1988, p. 50.

8. John Hoyt, *HSUS News* (Humane Society of the United States), Summer 1991.

9. HSUS Fact Sheet: "Puppy Mills" (Humane Society of the United States), undated.

10. Andrew Rowan, "Pet Overpopulation: The Problem and the Remedy," *Our Animal Wards*, Fall 1991, p. 10.

11. Wayne Pacelle, response to question on panel, Illinois Agricultural Leadership Foundation Conference, Washington, D.C., March 10, 1993. Pacelle later claimed to have been referring to farm animals only, but the question he was answering was "What about domestic animals?" That includes pets.

12. Hoyt, op. cit. Hoyt continued: "Adopt, and only adopt, until there is not one animal languishing in the shelters and pounds across the face of this country." Since most remaining animals euthanized in shelters today are too old, sick, or dangerous to be adoptable, this in effect means no more breeding at all, until dogs and cats become extinct.

13. The New Jersey Animal Rights Alliance (NJARA), "Should Dogs Be Kept as Pets? NO!" *Good Dog!* February 1991, p. 20.

14. Bryant, op. cit.

15. Confidential source.

16. Ibid.

17. Ingrid Newkirk, "Just Like Us? Toward a Notion of Animal Rights," (symposium) *Harper's*, August 1988, p. 50.

18. PeTA Fact Sheet: "Companion Animals," People for the Ethical Treatment of Animals, undated.

Chapter 7

1. Janice Stott Henke, *Seal Wars! An American Viewpoint* (St. John's, Newfoundland: Breakwater, 1985), p. 69. See also Ron Arnold and Alan Gott-

lieb, *Trashing the Economy: How Runaway Environmentalism Is Wrecking America* (Bellevue, Washington: Free Enterprise Press, 1993), p. 182.

2. Moira Welsh, "Indian Children Choosing Death as the Only Way Out," *Toronto Star*, January 30, 1993, p. A1. See also Tom Harpur, "Once-Proud Innu Robbed of the Will to Live," *Toronto Star*, February 7, 1993, p. A14.

3. Ellen Hopkins, "Animal Rights," *Newsday*, February 21, 1988, p. 24.

4. As cited by William C. Symonds, "Now, the Trapper Is an Endangered Species," *Business Week*, May 6, 1991, p. 24A.

5. John Barber, "The Persecution of the Fur Trade," *Reader's Digest* (Canadian Edition), August 1991, p. 37.

6. PeTA Factsheet, Wildlife #2, "Trapping: Pain for Profit," People for the Ethical Treatment of Animals, Washington, D.C., undated.

7. As cited in Tony Zappia, "Something Scary: There's an Anti-Trapping Bill," *Watertown Daily Times*, May 17, 1992, p. G8.

8. Untitled, undated publication from Friends of Animals, Norwalk, Connecticut.

9. John Barber, op. cit.

10. *Toronto Star*, August 6, 1986.

11. The Animal Liberation Front, "Reforming the Fur Industry, ALF Style," *Earth First! Journal*, Easter 1992, p. 7.

Chapter 8

1. "Ape Trainer Wins Suit Against Rights Group," *New York Times*, August 13, 1990, p. A12. See also Rod and Patti Strand, *The Hijacking of the Humane Movement* (Wilsonville, Oregon: Doral, 1992), p. 103; and Ron Arnold and Alan Gottlieb, *Trashing the Enonomy: How Runaway Environmentalism Is Wrecking America* (Bellevue, Washington: Free Enterprise Press, 1993), p. 423.

2. "Berosini Awarded $4.2 Million," *Las Vegas Review-Journal/Sun*, August 12, 1990, p. 5A.

3. "Berosini: Suspended!" *PeTA News*, July/August 1990.

4. "Berosini: Digging in Deeper," *PeTA News*, September/October 1990, p. 24.

5. "Absence of Malice: The Berosini Trial," *PeTA News*, September/October 1990, p. 24.

6. Longhorn World Championship Rodeo, "A Study Guide to Rodeo and the American Cowboy," undated.

7. The Humane Society of the Saginaw County, undated leaflet. Cf. PeTA Factsheet, "Rodeo: Cruelty for a Buck," Washington, D.C., undated.

8. Laura Hillenbrand, "Beyond All Reproach," *Equus*, No. 157 (1990), p. 78.

9. Glenn Emery, "Rodeo Folks Say Charge of Cruelty Is a Bum Steer," *Washington Times*, April 16, 1990, p. E1.

10. International Professional Rodeo Association, "The Care and Protection of Rodeo Livestock" (Pauls Valley, Oklahoma), undated.

11. Vicki Hearne, "What's Wrong with Animal Rights," *Harper's*, September 1991, p. 61.

12. Lyda Longa, "Hollywood Bans Animals in Circus," *Sun-Sentinel*, January 31, 1991.

13. Karen Asis, "Zoos and Aquariums: Sharing the Animal Welfare Commitment," *Psychologists for the Ethical Treatment of Animals Bulletin*, Spring 1990.

14. Gary G. Clarke, "Zoo Behavior: Animals and Visitors," *Kansas School Naturalist*, Vol. 28, No. 3 (February 1982), p. 6.

15. Ibid.

16. Lloyd Kiff, "To the Brink and Back: The Battle to Save the California Condor," *Terra*, Vol. 28, No. 4 (Summer 1990), p. 11. Cf. The Resources Agency of the Department of Fish and Game, State of California, "Status of the California Condor Program," June 19, 1991.

17. Asis, op. cit.

18. Letter from New England Aquarium, as cited in "Aquarium Sues Animal Cults," *The People's Agenda*, October 1991, p. 5.

19. The activist was "Cat" Kubic. She was arrested July 1991. Personal communication from the carriage driver she attacked is confidential.

20. "Horse Yes, PeTA NO," *Washington City Paper*, December 15, 1991.

Chapter 9

1. Richard Conniff, "Fuzzy-Wuzzy Thinking About Animal Rights," *Audubon*, November 1990, p. 132.

2. Aldo Leopold, *A Sand County Almanac and Sketches Here and There* (New York: Oxford University Press, 1949).

3. José Ortega y Gasset, *Meditations on Hunting*, trans. by Howard B. Wescott (New York: Charles Scribner's Sons, 1972).

4. Luke Dommer, fund-raising letter, Committee to Abolish Sport Hunting, February 15, 1990. As quoted in Russ Carman, *The Illusions of Animal Rights* (Iola, Wisconsin: Krause, 1990), p. 58.

5. Frank D. Roylance, "Deer Threaten Park's Ecosystem," *Baltimore Evening Sun*, March 5, 1991, p. A4. Cf. Pat Durkin, "Deer Threaten Park's Ecoystem," *Altoona Mirror*, January 6, 1991.

6. Wayne Pacelle, "Stop Slaughtering Yellowstone Bison," *USA Today*, January 8, 1991, p. 10A.

7. Actually, American hunters as a group are solidly middle class. See Alan Farnham, "A Bang That's Worth Ten Billion Bucks," *Fortune*, March 9, 1992, p. 80.

8. Daniel J. Decker and Tommy L. Brown, "How Animal Rightists View the 'Wildlife Management-Hunting System,'" *Wilderness Society Bulletin*, Vol. 15 (1987), p. 599.

9. Margaret L. Knox, "The Rights Stuff," *Buzzworm: The Environmental Journal*, 3, No. 3 (May/June 1991).

10. Michael Specter, "Cost of Princeton Tolerance: Deer," *Washington Post*, February 12, 1991, p. A3.

11. Walter E. Howard, "Wildlife Should Be Managed, Not Overprotected," *Bear-People Conflicts: Proceedings of A Symposium on Management Stategies*, ed. M. Bromley, April 6–10, 1987, Yellowknife, Northwest Territories, Canada, p. 216.

12. William ("Fossil Bill") Kramer ("The Angry Environmentalist"), "Cage People—Not Animals," *The People's Agenda*, May 1991, p. 10.

13. *Amherst Bee*, March 16, 1988.

Chapter 10

1. Carol L. Burnett, PeTA director of communications, as quoted in the University of Alabama *Crimson White*, April 3, 1989.

2. Chris DeRose, director, Last Chance for Animals, as quoted in *Santa Barbara News-Press*, April 12, 1988.

3. Katie McCabe, "Beyond Cruelty," *Washingtonian*, Vol. 25, No. 5 (February 1990), p. 76.

4. Dean Galbreath, "Mary McEachron Uses Her Legal Skills to Create Center on Aging," *San Francisco Business Times*, November 1, 1991.

5. Ibid.

6. German propaganda magazine cited in Christopher Paul Roberts, "National Socialism and the Modern Animal Rights Movement:

Some Interesting Parallels" (Northeastern University, 1990), as quoted in David R. Zimmerman, "Activists Use Anti-Semitic Tactics," *Probe*, June 1, 1992, p. 6.

7. Theodor G. Morell, *The Secret Diaries of Hitler's Doctor*, ed. David Irving (New York: Macmillan, 1983), p. 25.

8. John Toland, *Adolf Hitler* (Garden City, N.Y: Doubleday, 1976), p. 256.

9. Barnaby J. Feder, "Pressuring Purdue," *New York Times Magazine*, November 26, 1989, p. 32.

10. Walter C. Langer, *The Mind of Adolf Hitler* (New York: Signet, 1972), pp. 83–84.

11. As cited in Walter E. Howard, *Animal Rights vs. Nature* (Davis, California: Walter Howard, 1990), pp. 15–16.

12. Hermann Göring, "A Broadcast Over the German Radio Network Describing the Fight Against Vivisection and the Measures Taken to Prohibit It," August 28, 1933, *The Political Testament of Hermann Göring*, trans. H.W. Blood-Ryan (London: John Long, 1939), p. 73.

13. Cf. R. Waite, *The Psychopathic God* (New York: Basic Books, 1977), p. 41.

14. Arnold Arluke and Boria Sax, "Understanding Nazi Animal Protection and the Holocaust," *Anthrozöos*, Vol. 5, No. 1 (1992), p. 19.

15. William L. Shirer, *The Rise and Fall of the Third Reich* (New York: Simon and Schuster, 1959), pp. 979–991.

16. Peter Singer, *Animal Liberation: A New Ethic for our Treatment of Animals*, 2nd ed. (New York: The New York Review of Books, 1990), p. 85.

17. McCabe, op. cit., p. 192.

18. As quoted in Richard Conniff, "Fuzzy-Wuzzy Thinking About Animal Rights," *Audubon* (November 1990), p. 128.

19. See Chap. 1, Endnote 1 of this book.

20. B. P. Robert Stephen Silverman, *Defending Animals' Rights Is the Right Thing to Do* (New York: Shapolsky, 1992), p. 1. The "B. P." stands for "Buddy Pompie." The author legally changed his name to name himself after his two dogs, Buddy and Pompie.

21. Chip Brown, "She's a Portrait of Zealotry in Plastic Shoes," *Washington Post*, November 13, 1983, p. B10.

22. Boria and Sax, op. cit., p. 21.

23. Letter from Susan Rosenbluth, *The People's Agenda*, October 1991, p. 7.

24. Oscar Kraines, "Kashrut and the Constitution," *Midstream*, Vol. 38, No. 6 (August/September 1992), p. 29.

25. Ibid., p. 31.

26. "Animal Activists Adopt Anti-Semitic Tactics," *Jewish Voice and Opinion*, Vol. 3, No. 8 (April 1990), p. 12.

27. Ibid.

28. David Zimmerman, "Activist Hate Letters Contain Anti-Semitic Threats," *Probe*, June 1, 1992, p. 5.

29. Ibid.

30. Ibid.

31. David T. Hardy, "America's New Extremists: What You Need to Know About the Animal Rights Movement" (Washington, D.C.: Washington Legal Foundation, 1990), pp. 50–51, fn. 100.

32. Ibid.

33. Paul Watson, as quoted in *The Kitchener-Waterloo Record*, November 12, 1987.

34. Sydney Singer, *The Earth Religion* (Grass Valley, California: ABACE Publications, 1991), p. 57.

35. Ibid., p. 58.

36. Robert James Bidinotto, "Animal Rights: A New Species of Egalitarianism," *The Intellectual Activist*, September 14, 1983, p. 3.

37. Arluke and Sax, op. cit., p. 11.

38. Sydney Singer, "The Neediest of All Animals," *The Animals' Agenda*, Vol. 10, No. 5 (June 1990), p. 50.

39. "Screaming Wolf" (pseudonym), *A Declaration of War: Killing People to Save Animals and the Environment* (Grass Valley, California: Patrick Henry Press, 1991), p. 16.

40. Koppel S. Pinson, *Modern Germany: Its History and Civilization* (New York: Macmillan, 1954), p. 490.

41. As quoted in Peter Singer, op. cit., p. 7.

42. Sydney Singer, *The Earth Religion*, op. cit., pp. 18, 24–25.

43. Hermann Rauschning, *The Voice of Destruction* (New York: Putnam's, 1940), p. 222.

44. Marti Kheel, "Nature and Feminist Sensitivity," in Tom Regan and Peter Singer, eds., *Animal Rights and Human Obligations*, 2nd ed, (Englewood Cliffs, N.J.: Prentice Hall, 1989), p. 261.

45. Ibid.

46. Ibid., p. 262.

47. Josephine Donovan, "Animal Rights," *Signs: Journal of Women in Culture and Society*, Winter 1990, p. 365.

48. Ibid.

49. Peter Singer, as quoted in Donovan, op. cit., p. 357.

50. James Rachels, "Vegetarianism and 'The Other Weight Problem,' " *World Hunger and Moral Obligation*, William Aiken and Hugh LaFollette, eds. (Englewood Cliffs, N.J.: Prentice-Hall, 1977), pp. 180–193.
51. Clifton Perry, "We Are What We Eat," *Environmental Ethics*, Vol. 3 (Winter 1981), p. 345.
52. Tom Regan, *All That Dwell Therein* (Berkeley: University of California Press, 1982), pp. 202–203.
53. Tom Regan, "The Case for Animal Rights," in Peter Singer, ed., *In Defense of Animals* (New York: Harper and Row, 1986), p. 22.
54. Chris DeRose, as quoted in *Santa Barbara News-Press*, April 12, 1988.

BIBLIOGRAPHY

Books

Budiansky, Stephen. *The Covenant of the Wild: Why Animals Chose Domestication.* New York: William Morrow, 1992. An immensely readable and fascinating exploration of the science of human and animal "coevolution." Exposes animal rights as utterly ignorant of science and the reality of animals.

Carman, Russ. *The Illusions of Animal Rights.* Iola, Wis.: Krouse Publications, 1990. A noted trapper and outdoor writer, repeatedly targeted by terrorist threats, explores the mysterious roots of the animal rights movement.

Cross, H. Russell, and Floyd M. Byers, eds. *Current Issues in Food Production: A Perspective on Beef as a Component in Diets for Americans.* College Station: Texas A & M University, April 1990. A scholarly exposé of the fallacies of John Robbins' *Diet for a New America.*

Henke, Janice. *Seal Wars! An American Viewpoint.* St. John's, Newfoundland: Breakwater Books, 1985. The history of the war against sealing— the campaign that opened the passage from environmental extremism to animal rights.

Henshaw, David. *Animal Warfare.* Glasgow: Fontana Paperbacks, 1989. The first in-depth study of animal rights extremism in Great Britain.

Howard, Walter E. *Animal Rights Vs. Nature.* Davis, Calif.: Walter E. Howard, 1990. A world-renowned wildlife ecologist systematically annihilates animal rights with science and good humor.

McDowell, R.E. *A Partnership for Humans and Animals.* Raleigh, N.C.: Kinnic Publishers, 1991. A short, scholarly overview of human-animal interaction around the world. Debunks animal rights.

Ray, Dixy Lee, with Lou Guzzo. *Trashing the Planet: How Science Can Help Us Deal with Acid Rain, Depletion of the Ozone, and Nuclear Waste (Among Other Things).* Washington, D.C.: Regnery Gateway, 1990. A debunking of myths asserted by groups speaking in the cause of protecting the environment. The book also describes many animal rights groups.

Regan, Tom. *The Case for Animal Rights*. Berkeley: University of California Press, 1983. A quasi-Kantian attempt to supplant the concept of moral agency in ethics with the quality of being "the subject of a life."

Rifkin, Jeremy. *Beyond Beef: The Rise and Fall of the Cattle Culture*. New York: Dutton, 1992. A rehash of John Robbins' charges, but focusing specifically on cattle—and without the spirit guides.

Robbins, John. *Diet for a New America: How Your Food Choices Affect Your Health, Happiness and the Future of Life on Earth*. Walpole, N.H.: Stillpoint, 1987. This book was "channeled" to the author by a giant pig and a giant cow. It claims that livestock farming and ranching cause disease, famine, and ecological degradation.

Screaming Wolf (pseud.). *A Declaration of War: Killing People to Save Animals and the Environment*. Grass Valley, Calif.: Patrick Henry Press, 1991. A manifesto advocating animal and environmental terrorism.

Singer, Peter. *Animal Liberation: A New Ethic for Our Treatment of Animals*, 2nd ed. New York: New York Review of Books, 1990. Often called "the bible of animal rights," the book is actually a "preference utilitarian" attack on the concept of rights itself.

Singer, Sydney. *The Earth Religion: Reawakening the Human Animal*. Grass Valley, Calif.: ABACE Publications, 1991. A trance-channeled book, denouncing Judeo-Christianity in favor of animal and nature worship.

Strand, Rod, and Patti Strand. *The Hijacking of the Humane Movement*. Wilsonville, Oreg.: Doral Publishing, 1993. How animal rights groups are staging "hostile takeovers" of local humane societies. The book is also a good history of the animal rights movement.

Articles and Reports

"Animal Activism: The New Pornography." *Who's Mailing What!*, 6 (July/Aug. 1990), 1–21. An eye-opening look at the big money in animal rights direct-mail fundraising.

Arluke, Arnold, and Boria Sax. "Nazi Animal Protection and the Holocaust." *Anthrozoös*, 5, No. 1 (1992), 4–31. A stunning work of scholarship, exploding once and for all the canard that devotion to animal rights implies compassion for people.

Bidinotto, Robert James. "Environmentalism: Freedom's Foe for the '90s." *Freeman*, 40 (Nov. 1990), 409–20. A critique of environmental extremism, including a section on animal rights, as the coercive utopian legacy of Rousseau.

Conniff, Richard. "Fuzzy-Wuzzy Thinking About Animal Rights," *Audubon*, 92 (Nov. 1990), 120-33. An environmentalist concludes that animal rights opposition to trapping is based on "ignorance of nature."

Goldberg, Alan M., and John M. Frazier. "Alternatives to Animals in Toxicity Testing." *Scientific American*, 261 (Aug. 1989), 24-30. Director, Center for Alternatives to Animal Testing (Johns Hopkins University), debunks claim that animal testing is unnecessary.

Hardy, David T. "America's New Extremists: What You Need to Know About the Animal Rights Movement" (Washington, D.C.: Washington Legal Foundation, 1990). The best exposé of PeTA's links to ALF.

Hubbell, John G. "The 'Animal Rights' War on Medicine." *Reader's Digest*, 136 (June 1990), 70–76. A popular description of PeTA and ALF attacks on research.

Hueston, Harry R., II. "Terrorism in the '90s: Battling the Animal Liberation Front." *Police Chief*, 52 (Sept. 1990), 52–54. A law-enforcement perspective on ALF crime.

Jamison, Wesley V., and William M. Lunch, "Rights of Animals, Perceptions of Science, and Political Activism: Profile of Animal Rights Activists," *Science, Technology, and Human Values*, 17 (Autumn 1992), 438-458. A survey of animal rights protestors at the 1990 March on Washington.

McCabe, Katie. "Beyond Cruelty." *Washingtonian*, 25 (Feb. 1990), 72–77, 185–187, 189–195. The exposé of PeTA and HSUS that earned its author a whopping lawsuit. A correction and clarification of this article was published in *Washingtonian* to settle that litigation.

_____. "Who Will Live, Who Will Die?," *Washingtonian*, 21 (August 1986), 112–118, 153–157. A hard look at PeTA's attacks on researchers and the patients who suffer from those attacks.

Newkirk, Ingrid, Gary Francione, Roger Goldman, and Arthur Caplan, "Just Like Us? Toward a Notion of Animal Rights." *Harper's*, 277 (Aug. 1988), 43–52. Noted ethicist Arthur Caplan gets Newkirk and Francione to expose their ideas about animal rights.

Oliver, Charles. "Liberation Zoology." *Reason*, 22 (June 1990), 22–27. An argument that animal rights theory is a veiled attack on human rights.

Rosenberger, Jack. "The Ugly Secret of Black Beauty Ranch." *The Village Voice*, 35 (Dec. 18, 1990), 39–42. Fund for Animals hypocrisy is exposed.

Spencer, Leslie, with Jan Bollwerk and Richard C. Morais. "The Not So Peaceful World of Greenpeace." *Forbes*, 148 (Nov. 11, 1991), 174-79. The mother of all exposés.

U.S. Cong., Office of Technology Assessment. *Technology Against Terrorism:*

Structuring Security. Washington, D.C.: Government Printing Office, 1992. The scientific research division of the U.S. Congress exposes the connection between ALF, PeTA, and PCRM.

White, Robert J. "The Facts About Animal Research." *Reader's Digest*, 132 (Mar. 1988), 127-32. A refutation of animal rights attacks on research.

INDEX